Macroeconomics for AS Level

2nd Edition

Andrew Threadgould

informe

For my daughters, Phoebe and Clara

And in loving memory of my son, Jacob

And for my wife, Sarah

© Anforme Ltd 2009
ISBN 978-1-905504-30-5

Anforme Ltd, Stocksfield Hall, Stocksfield, Northumberland NE43 7TN.

Typeset by George Wishart & Associates, Whitley Bay.
Printed by SPD Limited, Gateshead.

Contents

Chapter 1

The Macroeconomy

Wealth creation and the factors of production

Macroeconomics is the study of economic activity on a national or global scale. As such, it is concerned with major economic issues such as economic growth, unemployment, development, poverty and inflation.

A dictionary definition of economics usually refers to the creation and distribution of wealth, and in macroeconomics we examine the large scale processes which determine wealth and the mechanisms through which it can be shared by economic agents such as consumers, workers, firms, pressure groups, trade unions and the government.

An economy converts inputs (the factors of production of land, labour, capital and enterprise) into output (goods and services). The efficiency with which this occurs is known as productivity. The typical measure used is labour productivity: output per worker.

The total output of an economy can be shown on a **production possibility frontier** (PPF), also known as a production possibility boundary, production possibility curve or transformation curve.

Figure 1.1: The production possibility frontier

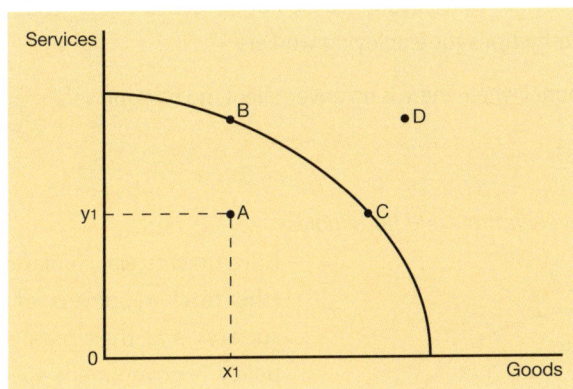

The PPF shows the combinations of goods and services which can be produced by the resources of this economy. All combinations of goods and services shown at points A, B and C are attainable because they are on or within the boundary. A point such as D, outside the PPF, is unattainable without an increase in the quantity and/or quality of the factors of production in the economy. A shift outwards of the PPF is called economic growth. The process by which this arises is a central concern for macroeconomists and a key determinant of the standard of living in an economy. Economic growth is the subject of Chapter 2.

As output could be higher than the x1 goods and y1 services produced at point A, there must be unused resources at this point. This is called **unemployment** and may result from underutilised land, spare machinery or office space or workers without jobs. Of key concern are unemployed workers: the problems associated with the jobless in an economy are extensive and harmful for both the unemployed and others. The issue of unemployment is discussed in much greater detail in Chapter 3.

The third big economic issue is that of **inflation**. In market-based economies firms produce goods and services which are then bought by households using the wages earned from work. This is called the circular flow of income. Producers of popular goods may be able to increase price to take advantage of strong demand; in periods where households are experiencing higher wages this may fuel an increase in the prices of most goods. This is inflation: a sustained increase in the general level of prices. Inflation is discussed further in Chapter 4.

The circular flow of income and economic agents

Macroeconomics examines the complex interaction between economic agents as they attempt to behave in a way which maximises their welfare. We can identify three main economic agents: consumers, firms and the government.

Consumers aim to maximise the utility, or satisfaction, they achieve from the goods and services they purchase. Workers aim to maximise their wages and other rewards from supplying their labour to firms. Households generally consist of both consumers and workers.

Firms aim to maximise profits: the difference between the cost of supplying goods and the revenue received from selling them. Trade unions aim to maximise the welfare of their members, and other pressure groups focus on the needs of their supporters, for example an environmental pressure group may aim to reduce the harm caused by pollution.

The government, in theory, aims to maximise social welfare: the total utility of all members of society. This assumption is questioned by some economists, as are the maximising behaviours set out above. Consumers may not always act rationally, and firms may not maximise profits if their managers choose instead to pursue their own objective of maximising their pay! Such conflict is at the heart of economics, but most economic theories assume that economic agents such as consumers, workers, firms and government act rationally, if not always predictably.

The relationship between firms and households is shown below in Figure 1.2.

The outer flow is a financial flow: income in the form of wages, and spending on goods and services are measured in monetary terms. The inner flow describes the physical flow. The flows run in opposite directions, showing the payments received for the supply of labour and goods and services, and each payment represents an income for the other agent. Consumption is also the revenue firms receive, and wages are also the costs incurred by firms for employing workers.

Figure 1.2 shows a very simple model where there is no government, no banking sector, and no international trade.

Figure 1.2: The circular flows between firms and households

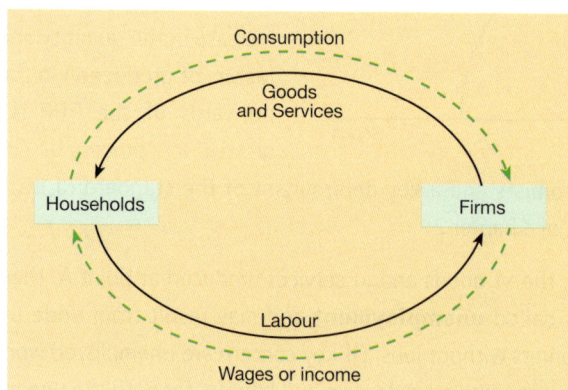

Governments aim to maximise social welfare (the total happiness of every person in society) and their main tool of economic policy is government spending, funded by either taxes or borrowing. In macroeconomic terms, the government therefore performs two main functions: they give money or services to households and firms (spending on public services such as transport, healthcare, education, defence and law and order, and welfare benefits), and they take money away from households and firms (taxation). The control of the budget position – the difference between government spending and taxation – is discussed further in Chapter 8.

Any wages, or income, not spent on consumption is called a withdrawal from the circular flow of income. Taxes are a major withdrawal from the circular flow; in the case of income tax this is usually deducted at source, i.e. directly from income through systems such as PAYE (Pay As You Earn). Another withdrawal is saving. Even after taxes, households do not (always) spend all they earn: they may also choose to save income for future spending. Savings enter the financial or banking sector of the economy, and banks use these funds to lend to other households (loans) or firms (to fund investment). Investment is capital spending by firms to increase their ability to supply goods and services; examples include building new factories or call centres, purchases of land, and training programmes for workers to increase their productivity. Where saving is a withdrawal, investment is an injection into the circular flow: it represents an increase in income in the economy by increasing the profits made by firms.

Similarly, not all flows remain within the domestic economy. Households, firms and the government in the UK may purchase imports of goods, services and raw materials from overseas, and foreign households, firms and governments purchase UK exports.

Imports represent a withdrawal and exports an injection. Chapter 5 looks in greater detail at the impact of imports and exports on the macroeconomy. The relative level of exports and imports is called the current account position.

According to the circular flow of income, the value of withdrawals will always equal the value of injections in an economy. This is shown in the two equations below:

Imports are a withdrawal from, and exports an injection into, the circular flow.

$Y = C + S + M + T$ (Equation 1)
Where Y = income, C = consumption, S = saving, M = imports and T = taxation

$Y = C + I + G + X$ (Equation 2)
Where Y and C still represent income and consumption, and I = investment, G = government spending and X = exports

Figure 1.3: Injections and withdrawals

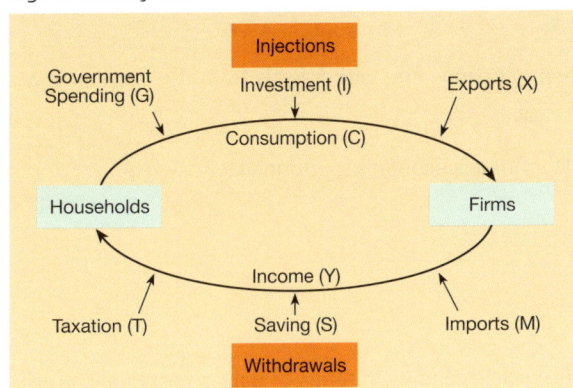

Equation 1 shows the uses of income: it is either spent on goods and services produced in the UK, saved, paid in taxes, or spent on imported goods and services. Equation 2 shows the sources of income: it is generated by consumption, from investment, government, or spending by foreigners.

These equations will be used more extensively in Chapter 6 when we examine the concept of aggregate demand.

Economic policy and economic performance

The performance of the macroeconomy has a huge impact on society. Growth, jobs and prices are central concerns of society and have fundamental impacts on our lives. Governments may be elected – or voted out of power – on the basis of the economic performance of the country. Bill Clinton once said, 'It's the economy, stupid', and all governments have a responsibility to try to tackle the key macroeconomic variables discussed above. Economic policy is central to political decision-making, and there are three main ways in which the economy can be managed.

Monetary policy seeks to control the amount and the value of money in the economy. In the 1980s governments in both the UK and USA sought to control the money supply – the notes, coins and proxy

monies available to households and firms to spend – in what was known as the Monetarist experiment, drawing heavily on the ideas of Milton Friedman and the Neo-Classical school of economics. In recent years monetary policy has been conducted through interest rates. Interest rates represent both a reward to savers and a cost to borrowers; changes in interest rates therefore shift the behaviour of households and firms. Monetary policy is discussed further in Chapter 7.

Chapter 8 looks at another demand management policy. **Fiscal policy** is the setting of taxes and spending levels by the government. Like monetary policy, fiscal policy affects the level of aggregate demand in the economy but whereas interest rates are determined monthly by the Monetary Policy Committee, the budget (the key tool of fiscal policy) is set annually by the Treasury, and is therefore under more direct government control.

The level of aggregate demand in the economy is crucial in determining how close to the PPF the economy is operating. The position of the PPF is determined by the quantity and quality of factors of production in the economy. The PPF represents the supply-side potential of the economy: the maximum combinations of all goods and services that could be produced if land, labour, capital and enterprise were fully utilised. This level can be influenced by **supply-side policy** and this will be explored in Chapter 9.

Chapter 10 will summarise key developments in the UK economy in recent years and review the links between macroeconomic variables, and explore some of the competing views on the economy which make the subject of macroeconomics so fascinating – and so contentious!

Summary questions

1. What do we mean by the macroeconomy?

2. Explain the importance of factors of production to the economy. How do they influence the basic economic problem of what, how and for whom to produce?

3. Explain why each of economic growth, unemployment and inflation has such an influence on the people in an economy.

4. What is the difference between injections and withdrawals from the circular flow of income? Use examples to explain your answer.

5. In what ways can governments influence economic performance?

Extension questions

A. Research the last ten years of the UK economy in terms of data on economic growth, inflation, unemployment, budget position and trade balance.

B. What are the key trends in the figures in question A? Are these measures rising, falling or constant at present?

C. Consider the major economies of the USA, Germany and China. Compare current data for the UK with figures for these other countries. What factors could account for these differences in economic performance?

Chapter 2

Economic Growth

Measuring economic growth

A major problem of studying economics is the way in which some concepts have more than one name. Similarly, some economic terms are often used imprecisely. Economic growth is a key example. Strictly speaking, economic growth refers to an increase in the productive capacity of the economy. This can be seen on Figure 2.1 below.

Figure 2.1: Economic growth

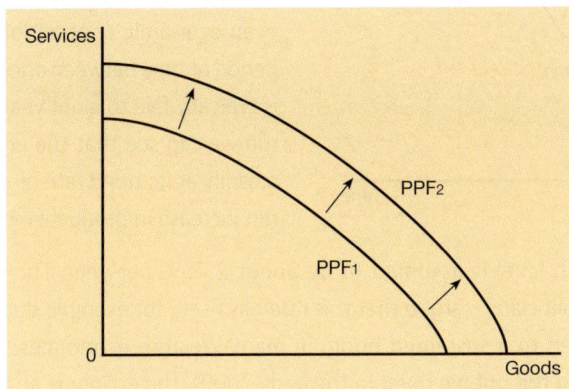

The shift from PPF1 to PPF2 is economic growth; an increase in the quantity and/or quality of factors of production which increases total potential output. The ways in which this could happen with respect to each of the factors of production include:

Land: land reclamation, or the discovery of stocks of fossil fuels or minerals; greater use of higher yield farming methods, more sophisticated technology to extract raw materials.

Labour: an influx of workers from overseas, previous increases in the birth rate feeding into the labour force, an increase in the retirement age; government training to increase the skills of the workforce.

Capital: higher investment in machinery, perhaps encouraged by cheaper finance; innovations in productive technologies.

Entrepreneurship: more extensive and/or more successful training for managers.

Figure 2.2: Unused productive potential

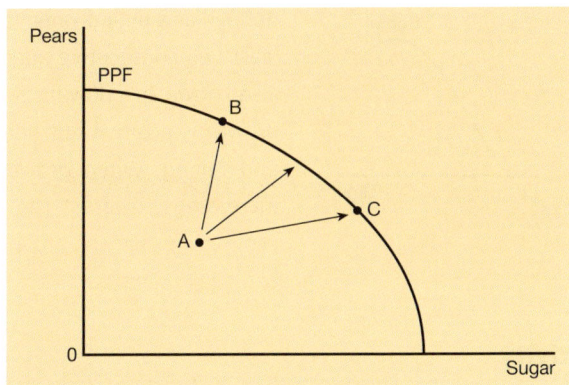

Problems arise when economists attempt to measure the growth rate of the economy. Productive potential is very difficult to identify and a proxy measure is **Gross Domestic Product** (GDP). GDP measures the total value of all output in the economy over a given period of time, usually a year. However, GDP measures actual output rather than productive potential. It is possible for an economy to operate inside the PPF if there is unemployment, also known as spare capacity.

Point A in Figure 2.2 shows such a position. The output of pears and/or sugar can be increased – to points B or C respectively, or any other point on the PPF – without any loss of the other good. Moving from a point inside the PPF to a point nearer the boundary therefore incurs no opportunity cost. The costs of

remaining within the PPF are explored in the next chapter when we consider unemployment in greater detail.

An increase in GDP may therefore arise through a shifting out of the PPF (economic growth) or through a movement nearer to the boundary (economic recovery). Similarly, output may fall because the PPF shifts inwards or because the economy is making less effective use of the resources available. To distinguish between these two effects economists sometimes refer to 'long-run' growth, to describe increases in the productive capacity of the economy, and 'short-run' growth, which refers to fluctuations in GDP resulting from changes in the level of economic activity. This is represented on Figure 2.3 which shows the economic cycle.

Figure 2.3: The economic cycle

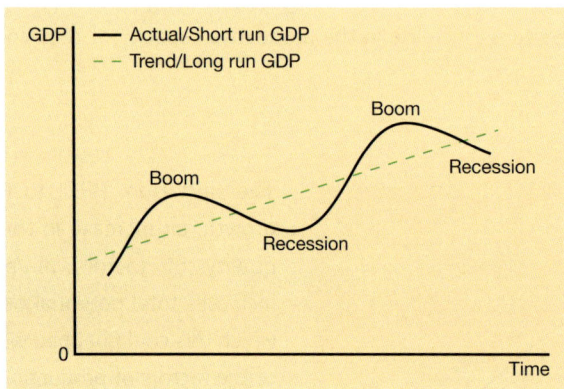

The **economic cycle**, also known as the **business cycle** or the **trade cycle**, shows the typical changes in the macroeconomy over time. Periods of rapid increases in GDP (boom) are balanced by periods of slower growth, or even economic contraction (recession). The period of time between one boom and another is typically five to eight years, but in the long-run we can see that the economy is growing steadily at its trend rate of growth – the long-run increase in productive capacity.

In the UK, the long-run growth level is assumed to be about 2.75% per year. There are times when economists – and particularly politicians – argue that this rate has risen, for example during the late 1990s when the internet revolution led to a sustained boom in many Western economies. Long-run growth projections were raised but when the bubble burst in the early 2000s, the economy appeared to return to its previous trend rates of growth.

Between booms and recessions economists identify periods of slowdown and upturn. This is more easily shown in Figure 2.4, where the vertical axis measures economic growth (% change in real GDP) rather than GDP.

Figure 2.4: Boom and recession

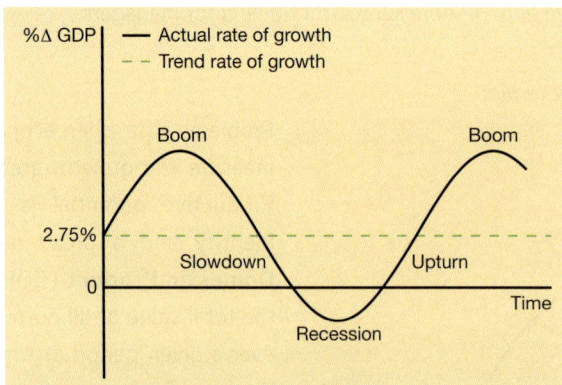

A *boom* is defined as a period of time during which real GDP increases at a faster rate than the trend rate of growth. A *recession* is defined as a period when real GDP falls for at least two consecutive quarters. A slowdown, also known as a downturn, is occurring when growth is positive but below the trend rate and falling. When growth is positive and increasing towards the trend rate the economy is enjoying an upturn or recovery.

Economic growth and productivity

Economic growth does not always occur uniformly across the economy. Figure 2.5 shows the case of an economy producing two goods: apples and films. The shift out to PPF2 represents an increase in the productivity of the apple industry. Note that the maximum output of films at point F (where all resources are used to make films and zero are used for apples) remains unchanged.

Figure 2.5: Uneven economic growth

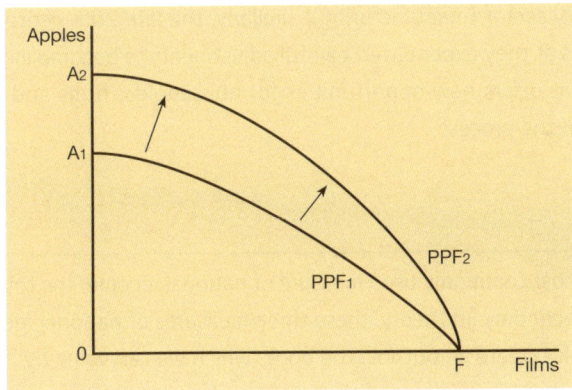

An increase in productivity in both industries, i.e. across the whole economy, would shift out the maximum possible quantity in both industries, creating a shift as seen in Figure 2.1.

Productivity measures output relative to input. In developed economies such as the UK or the USA the economic growth rate is closely linked to gains in productivity, most notably labour productivity. Labour productivity measures output per worker, and differences in this measure are a key factor in the differing growth rates seen across different economies.

Economic growth and economic development

Economic growth describes an increase in GDP and as we have seen above, we can distinguish between long-run and short-run growth. Economic development is different to growth in that it usually refers to structural changes in the economy which increase the long-run, productive potential of the economy. The internet boom of the late 1990s was mentioned above, and this was a period when new technologies and business models offered opportunities to firms and consumers alike. For a time, it could be argued, the long-run growth rate increased. When economists discuss development issues they usually refer to problems in less economically developed economies (LEDCs) such as poverty, aid and environmental issues. But more economically developed economies (MEDCs) also face issues related to development – and, of course, MEDCs have by definition experienced periods of development in the past. Examples include the industrial revolution (from the late 18th century onwards in Europe) where the main industry

The internet boom has helped increase economic growth.

in the economy, and therefore the main employer, shifted from the primary sector (agriculture and fossil fuel extraction) to the secondary sector (manufacturing); similarly, the late 20th century saw many more developed economies face crises as they experienced painful adjustments to become more tertiary (service sector) orientated. Development offers new opportunities for households, firms and governments, but may create winners and losers in the process.

GDP as a measure of growth

Gross Domestic Product is the most commonly used measure of national income: the total value of output, expenditure and income in the economy. In theory, these three measures of national income will be equal. For example, in writing this book I create an output (the book, which we can value by its selling price), an expenditure (your – or your teacher's – purchase of the book) and an income (the payment for the book to the publisher). Therefore if all such transactions across the economy were totalled, national output equals national expenditure equals national income.

However, GDP is not a perfect measure of living standards. The happiness (or welfare) of society is not simply a function of the spending and incomes of its people. We can easily identify a number of arguments against the use of GDP to measure welfare. We consider these in turn.

1. GDP takes no account of inflation

When I was an A level student I enjoyed an allowance from my parents of £5 per week. This may seem paltry by modern standards, but in the late 1980s a pint of beer cost less than £1 and a record (not yet a CD!) typically cost £3.99. Prices increase over time. Economists call this inflation (see Chapter 4) and this appears to undermine GDP as a way of comparing national income over time. In 1990 UK GDP was £558,160m and in 2003 this had risen to £1,110,296m. But did GDP really double? The figures suggest so, but the data is nominal: it takes no account of inflation. £1.1bn in 2003 is worth less than £1.1bn would have been worth in 1990 – simply because prices have risen in the meantime. Data adjusted for the effect of inflation is called 'real'. In fact, national income in 1990, if measured in 2003 prices, would be valued at £814,956. Real GDP has risen, therefore, but not by as much as nominal GDP. Real GDP growth was 36%, compared with nominal growth of 99%. This suggests that there was inflation and over time this eroded the spending power, or real value of household's incomes.

2. GDP takes no account of changes in population

Imagine a very simple economy based on hunter-gathering agriculture. If a tribe can catch 40 fish in a day, we need to know how many people this must feed before we judge whether the economy is successful or not. Population growth should increase GDP – assuming extra workers emerge and are employed. But the GDP per head (or per capita) may rise or fall, depending on the increase in output relative to the increase in population.

In the UK real GDP per capita rose from £14,238 to £18,644 between 1990 and 2003. This represents an increase of 31%. Thus, once the effects of higher prices and higher population have been taken into account the nominal growth of 99% falls to less than a third of that level.

3. GDP takes no account of unofficial work

This is a serious problem for statisticians: how can they measure unknown values? Output, and related income, may go undeclared as households avoid or limit their tax burden. Similarly, illegal activities (the shadow economy) will not be voluntarily brought to the attention of the government. Another issue is that of unpaid work. Households may care for elderly relatives and children and undertake DIY. If these activities were paid for – in payments to care homes, crèches and builders – this would increase measured GDP. Yet the work is done nonetheless and in any economy where such services are more likely to be provided by the household rather than a firm, GDP may be underestimated.

4. GDP takes no account of the changing quality of goods and services

This is also a problem. Back in 1990 when I listened to music while revising for my A level Economics exam, I did so on a tape deck, with all the accompanying background noise and inconvenience of turning the tape over half way through. Nowadays, you revise listening to an ipod with thousands of tunes at your disposal and a much higher sound quality. Home computers in 1990 were rare and laughably primitive – and expensive – when compared with a modern model. Similarly, the car industry has improved dramatically in recent years, with consumers benefiting from falling prices on higher quality products: a double gain. Yet GDP would measure this output lower due to the lower price, suggesting (erroneously) that the value of output has fallen.

5. GDP takes no account of other impacts on our standard of living (e.g. externalities)

Externalities occur when markets fail to fully account for the social impact of production and consumption. An economy may enjoy high levels of growth during periods

An iPod has increased the quality of listening to music compared to a tape deck.

of industrialisation, but this will come at a cost to the environment. Resource levels of fossil fuels may be depleted and the natural environment degraded by pollution from heavy industry and the growth of car ownership. If the market price of a good does not reflect these external costs then GDP, as a sum of all market prices, will similarly fail to account for the pollution created. When economists discuss sustainable growth this can mean the long-run trend level (sustainable economic growth), and/or the environmentally sustainable growth rate. An example is over-farming: high crop yields may be possible in the short-run but if continued, this could damage the soil permanently – resulting in lower yields in the future.

6. GDP data does not reflect income inequality

Real GDP per capita data shows average income per person. But the averaging process may mask inequality. Imagine a very simple economy with ten households and GDP of £400,000. The quality of life for the average citizen is very different if GDP is split equally (£40,000 per household) than if there is a high degree of inequality (one household with, say, an income of £310,000, and nine households earning £10,000 each). Thus any assessment of the average standard of living using GDP data requires an examination of modal and median income levels in addition to mean income.

7. Comparing GDP between economies requires an exchange rate

The exchange rate is the value of a currency in terms of another currency. When comparing, say, the GDP of France and the UK, it is necessary to convert French GDP from euros into sterling – or vice versa. But choosing the correct exchange to use can be problematic and potentially distorting. *The Economist* periodically publishes its Big Mac index, which compares prices between countries by using a uniform good – a burger.

Economic growth in the UK: 1990-2008

Figure 2.6 shows the rate of economic growth for the UK economy in recent years.

The UK economy last experienced a recession in 1991. Growth recovered throughout the 1990s and remained higher than the trend rate of 2.75% until 2001. The data shows why some economists proposed that the internet was fuelling a 'New Economic Paradigm' as the internet afforded new prospects for

Figure 2.6: UK Real GDP growth (% p.a.)

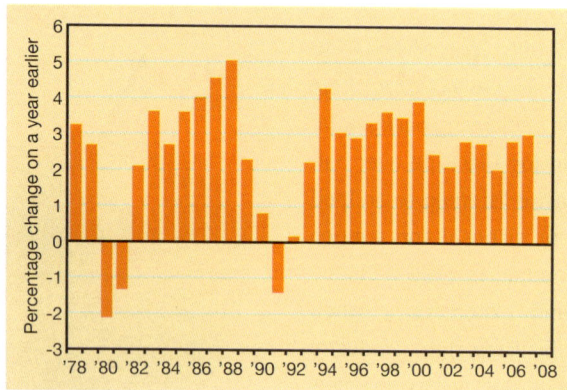

Source: www.hm-treasury.gov.uk

households and firms alike. By 2001, however (and even before the terrorist attacks in New York of 9/11) growth was cooling in both the UK and USA as the 'dot-com boom' ended and there was what economists call a 'readjustment' of the value of new technology companies in stock markets on both sides of the Atlantic.

In 2008 the UK economy entered recession.

Summary questions

1. Using a PPF diagram, distinguish between long-run economic growth and economic recovery.

2. What factors determine long-run, or trend, growth in an economy?

3. How does economic growth differ from economic development?

4. Why do economists prefer to use real GDP per capita to measure living standards?

5. What problems, other than inflation and population changes, could arise from using GDP data to compare living standards (a) over time, and (b) between countries?

Extension questions

A. In the late 1990s economists in major economies such as the UK and USA referred to the 'New Economic Paradigm': an upward shift in the trend rate of growth? Why does new technology such as the internet affect economic growth in this way?

B. What causes recessions? Why do economies tend to follow a 'boom-bust' pattern over time?

C. How clear is the link between economic growth and negative externalities such as pollution and social problems? Does this provide an argument for limiting economic growth or are more specific policies (tackling pollution and the impact of inequality) more appropriate?

Chapter 3

Unemployment

Unemployment as an economic problem

Unemployment is arguably the most damaging of economic problems to face an economy. The jobless endure personal hardship and poverty, the economy as a whole experiences a lower output level than is possible, and government funds are diverted into welfare payments to support the unemployed and their families.

Unemployment can be thought of as the difference between job creation and job losses. In a dynamic economy there will be continuous changes to industrial structure and – in an increasingly globalised economy – movements of production and supply across international borders. This results in both job losses, leading to increases in unemployment, and job creation, which reduces unemployment. Unemployment will rise when job losses outweigh job creation, and fall when the opposite occurs.

Measuring unemployment

Unemployment can be measured as a total value (e.g. 3 million unemployed) or as a percentage of the workforce. The latter is more useful when comparing unemployment both across different countries (where populations and workforce sizes may differ) and over time (when population levels may rise or fall).

Unemployment occurs when a person is willing and able to work but cannot find a job and is actively seeking one. Different measures of unemployment use slightly difference definitions.

There are two main measures of unemployment. The first is the **Labour Force Survey** (LFS). This surveys a large number of households (60,000) and is based on the definition of unemployment from the International Labour Organisation (ILO). The LFS generally produces a higher unemployment figure than the second measure, called the **Claimant Count** (CC). The CC counts the number of people claiming unemployment benefits, and to be eligible for unemployment benefit in the UK a person must be 'actively seeking work'.

The main reason why a survey of households uncovers a larger number of people who want to work than those claiming benefits is that of benefit eligibility. Some people have not paid enough national insurance contributions to be eligible to receive benefits, and some households may have a high enough income from working members or private pensions (e.g. early retirees) to remove eligibility for benefits from those who would work if the opportunity arose.

Causes and types of unemployment

The main factor determining the level of employment, and therefore unemployment, is the level of economic activity in the economy. GDP and changes in GDP (economic growth) have a strong influence on the demand for workers. When the quantity of goods and services produced is below the potential level (see Figure 3.1, point A) then there is not enough work for all factors of production to be fully employed.

The shortfall in production (the output of both goods and services is lower than is possible) leads to a shortfall in the need for workers – hence unemployment. The demand for all factors of production is a derived demand: firms employ resources, including labour, to produce goods and services. Therefore if firms are producing lower output levels, they will lay off workers and unemployment will rise.

Figure 3.1: Unemployed resources

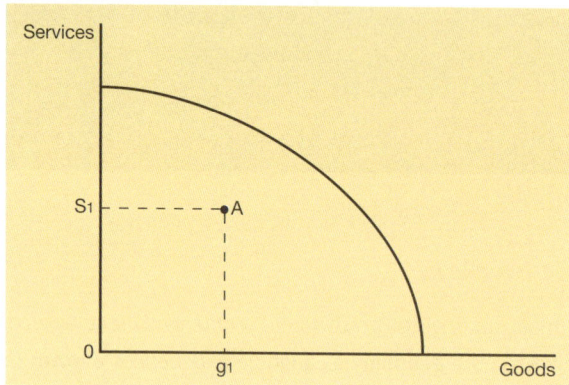

This type of unemployment is called **demand-deficient unemployment**. It is caused by short-run fluctuations in aggregate demand and rises rapidly during the recession and slowdown stages of the economic cycle (it is also known as cyclical unemployment).

However, even during a boom there may be people without jobs. The reasons causing this represent the other types of unemployment.

Frictional unemployment results when workers are not able to perfectly synchronise leaving one job with starting another, and for the period in between they are unemployed. Frictional unemployment will exist even during periods of rapid economic growth, but it will tend to be higher when the economy is growing more slowly. It is also called search unemployment.

Closely related to frictional unemployment is **seasonal unemployment**. Some sectors of the industry traditionally make use of casual workers and at particular times of the year firms cut production and release workers. Construction, agriculture and tourism are typical examples of industries which contribute to seasonal fluctuations in job creation and job losses.

Structural unemployment creates a long-term issue for the economy. It arises from a mismatch between the skills of workers and the jobs available. The structurally unemployed wish to work but their skills, experience and qualifications do not meet the needs of firms. Structural unemployment occurs when the pattern of production changes in an economy, for example during periods of industrialisation and deindustrialisation. In the 1970s and early 1980s unemployment was rising in the UK, partly because of recession and economic crisis, but also due to the decline in traditionally important industries such as mining and manufacturing. Jobs were lost in the primary and secondary sectors and created in the tertiary

Migrant workers picking strawberries. Agriculture gives rise to seasonal unemployment.

sector, and redundant miners and steelworkers did not have the right skills to work in the burgeoning finance and IT sectors. Where physical capital (machines) replace human capital (workers), for example when manufacturers make more intensive use of automated processes, economists use the term technological unemployment to describe the resulting loss of jobs.

Long-term unemployment may result from structural and technological unemployment. One theory suggests that the longer a person is out of work, the harder it becomes to find work as their skills become out-dated and they lose confidence and become less attractive to employers. This may occur during a prolonged recession, perhaps blurring the distinction between cyclical and structural unemployment. In addition, structural unemployment tends to be concentrated in areas traditionally associated with a particular industry, causing geographical unemployment.

Figure 3.2: Labour market equilibrium

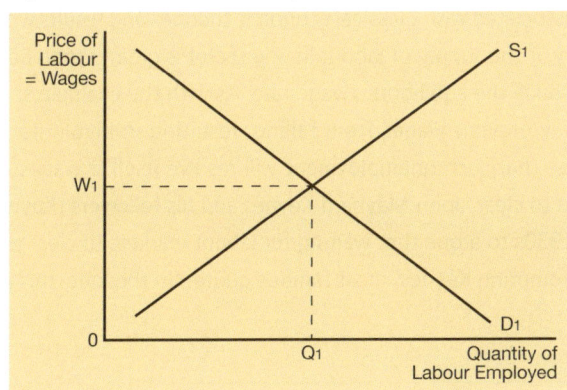

Economists also distinguish between **voluntary** and **involuntary unemployment**. Figure 3.2 shows a labour market where D1 shows the demand by firms for labour. S1 represents the supply, by households, of workers. The equilibrium price of labour is the wage rate in this particular industry.

At equilibrium employment level Q1 there is still some unemployment. The workers on the supply curve above point A are unable or unwilling to work at the market wage rate of W1 and are classed as voluntarily unemployed: they choose not to work for the prevailing wage rate.

Many economists dispute how quickly labour markets clear. In reality, workers may receive wages above the market wage rate due to imperfections in the labour market. Despite the name, such imperfections may benefit people who have jobs. Figure 3.3 shows a market where workers are paid W2, a wage rate above the equilibrium level. Workers may be able to negotiate above-equilibrium wages through collective bargaining (trade union power), long-term contracts and employment protection legislation, or because firms see an advantage in paying relative high wages (perhaps to reduce staff turnover, increase motivation, or to attract the most able workers in the industry). Minimum wage legislation, designed to protect low earners, may actually create unemployment by reducing the quantity of labour demanded.

Figure 3.3: Involuntary unemployment

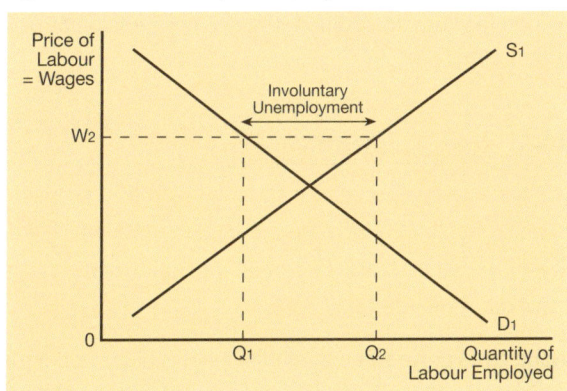

The wage rate W2 attracts a higher supply of workers to the industry: Q2 workers are willing and able to work now. However, as the cost of employing workers is higher, firms will only employ Q1 workers. (Q2 − Q1) is involuntary unemployment. These workers want to work for W2 but they cannot find a job. (Note that those people above Q2 are still classed as voluntary unemployment). Because the market is operating away from equilibrium (supply is permanently above demand at wage W2) firms will have to select workers through non-wage factors, such as family connections, waiting lists (economists sometimes refer to wait unemployment as a form of frictional unemployment: people

waiting for a better job than those currently available) or implicit and explicit discrimination. Thus equal opportunities legislation may be regarded as particularly important in an economy where labour markets are particularly inflexible and susceptible to imperfection.

Hidden unemployment is, arguably, not actually unemployment at all. The term can be used to refer to those people who do not figure in measures such as the claimant count, but it can also describe underemployment: the employment of high-skills workers in low-skill jobs. This under-utilisation of the full human capital of the workforce represents a loss not only to the economy – higher value output would be possible if the worker was more suitably employed – but also to the individual in terms of lower income. Some sectors of the workforce may be particularly susceptible to underemployment, such as working mothers (who may take lower-skill jobs to balance family and work commitments), students (e.g. seasonal employment in agriculture, manufacturing and hospitality) and retirees (e.g. pensioners on their 'second-careers' in retail and the caring professions).

Real wage unemployment is associated with Classical economic theories and results when labour markets do not clear effectively. In theory, if the supply of labour in one sector is greater than demand (i.e. if there is unemployment) this should reduce the equilibrium wage rate. As with the example shown in Figure 3.3, labour market imperfections may prevent wages from falling, resulting in involuntary unemployment. Classical economists would argue that such unemployment will resolve itself if wages are allowed to fall and the labour market is allowed to clear. John Maynard Keynes and his followers (Keynesian economists) drew on the experience of the 1930s to argue that waiting for labour markets to clear potentially involves a prolonged period of misery, prompting Keynes' most famous quote: 'In the long-run we're all dead'.

The costs of unemployment

For individual workers and their families, unemployment will, in the long-run, cause poverty. Unemployment benefits are lower than earned income and this gap reflects the limited lifestyle options, an inability to save, and possible long-term dependence on government support.

As unemployment tends to concentrate geographically (even within an area of low unemployment), there is the possibility of social problems associated with poverty and low aspirations. There may be disaffection with the limited prospects for young people in these areas, resulting in a low uptake of educational and training opportunities and economic costs related to policing, welfare and high healthcare costs.

For the economy as a whole there is lost output. Producing inside the PPF implies there are fewer goods and services available for either domestic consumption or exporting overseas. Higher supply would result in lower prices for consumers and a stronger position on the current account.

Most governments are committed to a welfare system which uses tax revenues to fund unemployment benefits. Welfare benefits are an example of transfer payments: spending which does not result in an output. Fiscal drag arises as the unemployed receive funds which could otherwise be used to improve infrastructure, education or recreation facilities. In addition, the unemployed do not pay taxes, resulting in a double loss to the government budget.

The benefits of unemployment?

Despite the huge human and economic costs associated with high levels of unemployment, an economy with a pool of available workers would be able to increase production quickly to take advantage of new opportunities in both domestic and global markets. Frictional unemployment is often regarded as an essential lubricant to the labour market in the economy.

Firms may also be able to keep wage costs down when unemployment is high: workers are far less likely to take industrial action or pursue high wage increases when they feel they could be easily replaced. It is possible, if not inevitable, that these lower costs may be passed onto consumers as lower prices, and low wages may also help the economy to remain competitive in export markets.

Government policy on unemployment

Unemployment is a serious issue for any economy and as such it is a central concern for policy-makers. There are two broad policies used to tackle unemployment, and they are covered in greater detail in Chapters 7, 8 and 9.

Demand management policy aims to stabilise the macroeconomy over the economic cycle. The government intervenes to increase aggregate demand during a slowdown and recession. By supplementing household demand the government aims to ensure that firms do not need to cut output, and thus employment levels, so quickly. Thus unemployment rises more slowly. Chapters 7 and 8 describe how fiscal and monetary policy can be used to control cyclical unemployment.

Supply-side policies aim to increase the willingness and ability of firms and government to produce and provide goods and services. Structural unemployment can be tackled through retraining opportunities and regional policy and improved rights to working mothers can help

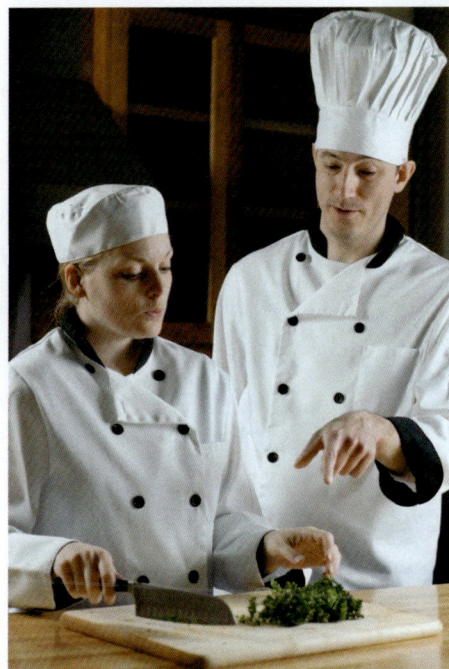

Structural unemployment can be tackled through retraining.

to prevent underemployment. Modern economies strive to create a flexible workforce where workers can easily move between industries, minimising frictional and technological unemployment in the process. Workers with transferable skills have the education and skills necessary for a wide range of work. This may be particularly true where the dominant sector in the economy is the service industry (as is the case for the UK) where literacy, numeracy, ICT and interpersonal skills may be more important than specific experience.

Unemployment in the UK: 1990-2008

Figure 3.4: UK unemployment, millions

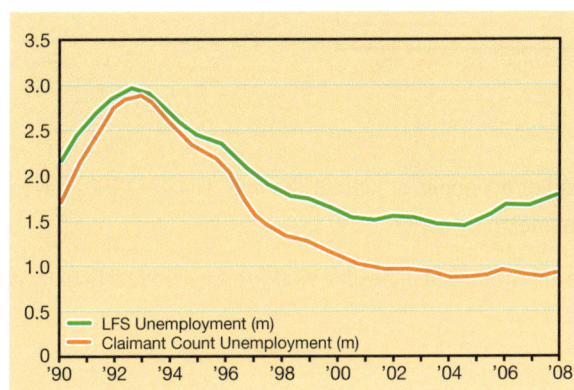

Source: www.hm-treasury.gov.uk

Figure 3.4 shows the trends in both Labour Force Survey (LFS) unemployment and the Claimant Count (CC) for the UK between 1990 and 2008. Both measures of unemployment rose in the early 1990s as the economy experienced recession, before falling steadily throughout the economic recovery and boom from 1993 onwards. Annual data for 2008 shows a reverse of this trend as both measures show rapid increases in unemployment for the first time in over a decade. This continued into 2009 with LFS unemployment rising to 2.4 million and CC to 1.56 million.

Summary questions

1. Why does the Labour Force Survey measure unemployment as higher than the Claimant Count?

2. Distinguish between demand-side and supply-side causes of unemployment.

3. In the UK economy in 2008, why may structural rather than cyclical factors help to explain the persistence of unemployment of almost 1 million (even using the lowest measure)?

4. How may demand management measures such as fiscal and monetary policy be used to reduce cyclical unemployment?

5. "Unemployment is always the result of low economic growth." To what extent do you agree with this statement?

Extension questions

A. Figure 3.5 shows long-term unemployment in the UK in recent years, both for workers unemployed for more than 18 months and for more than 24 months. What factors cause long-term unemployment?

Figure 3.5: Long-term unemployment in UK, thousands

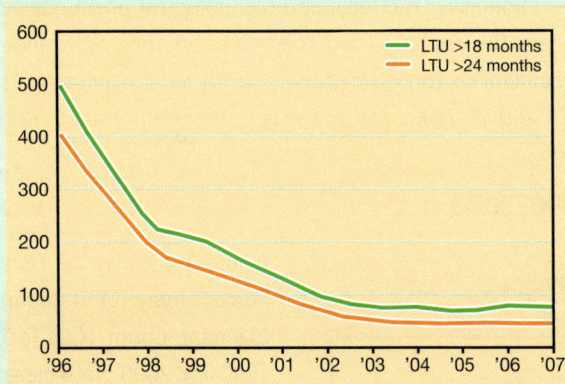

Source: www.hm-treasury.gov.uk

B. Why may the prolonged period of economic growth in the mid- to late-1990s have contributed to a falling level of long-term unemployment?

C. Why do economists stress the importance of a 'flexible workforce' when tackling unemployment?

Chapter 4

Inflation

Inflation as an economic problem

Inflation is defined as a sustained increase in the general level of prices. Whereas unemployment and the resulting poverty has obvious and direct consequences for those people and households affected, it could be argued that rising prices, although inconvenient, represent a lesser problem. This is not the case. Even in cases less extreme then the hyper-inflation experienced in Germany in the 1920s (which necessitated the creation of a new currency) inflation causes problems and a loss of welfare. More recently, economies such as Brazil and Argentina suffered in the 1980s with dangerously high levels of inflation.

UK inflation increased above 5% during 2008 (mainly due to high energy prices) and although this figure is not dramatic enough to be compared with hyperinflation in Germany and Latin America, it still created problems and a dilemma for UK policy-makers.

Measuring inflation

In December 2003 the UK moved from using the RPI (Retail Price Index) to the **CPI** (**Consumer Price Index**) as the primary measure of inflation. Both measures select a basket of goods which reflects the typical spending of an average household over a given period of time. The total spending on this range of goods and services is collected monthly and an inflation figure is calculated. Inflation is usually expressed as an annual change, thus the total spending in June 2007 will be compared to the figure for June 2006. If the total price of the basket of goods has risen by 3% over the year, this corresponds to an annual inflation figure of 3%.

Figure 4.1: UK inflation (CPI and RPI), % p.a.

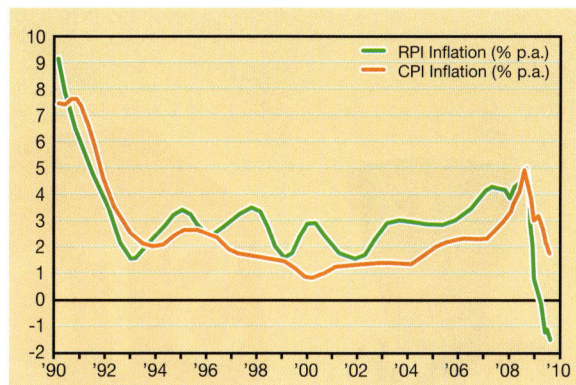

Source: www.hm-treasury.gov.uk

Figure 4.1 shows the CPI inflation rate from 1990 onwards. Note that between 2003, when the CPI was adopted as the official measure of inflation and February 2007, inflation did not move outside the target boundaries of 1% to 3%.

In March 2007 CPI inflation briefly rose above its target of 3%, and after rising throughout 2008 reached 5.2% in September. CPI fell below 3% in March 2009, the same month that the RPI measure became negative, showing deflation in the UK economy for the first time in many years. The implications of a movement outside the target range are explored further in Chapter 7.

The main difference between the two inflation measures most commonly used in the UK is the inclusion of mortgage interest payments and housing depreciation in the RPI, prices which are excluded from the CPI. RPIX (Retail Price Index excluding mortgage interest payments) was used in the UK until 2003 until CPI became the main measure used by the Bank of England for inflation targeting.

Causes and types of inflation

Demand-pull inflation arises when aggregate demand grows more quickly than the ability of firms to supply more goods and services. The higher spending in the economy results in upward pressure on prices.

Cost-push inflation arises from firms facing higher costs for their inputs. As factors of production become more expensive firms must increase prices to maintain profit margins.

Sometimes demand-pull and cost-push factors combine in what is called a wage-price spiral. As the cost of living increases, workers push for higher pay increases to maintain real income levels. These higher wages increase firms' costs and fuel inflationary pressure, causing even higher wage demands in the future. In extreme cases this process persists and causes hyper-inflation.

Some economists argue that the phenomenon of very high levels of inflation (at the peak of the problem in Germany in the 1920s prices were doubling every 49 hours) results from inadequate government control of the money supply. The money supply is the total value of notes and coins in circulation. If the government prints money to cope with an economic crisis, the increase in the money supply bids up prices and the currency rapidly becomes worth less, and in extreme cases worthless! This is called monetary inflation and is a fundamental belief of the Monetarist School of economics.

The costs of inflation

High levels of inflation reduce confidence in the economy and may therefore reduce investment. Firms as well as households find it difficult to predict the future and will make as few long-run plans as possible. This harms economic growth in both the short-run (investment is a component of aggregate demand) and the long-run (investment shifts out the productive potential of the economy by increasing the quality and/or quantity of factors of production).

In addition, the price mechanism performs an important function in allocating and rationing resources and sending signals to consumers and firms; thus rapid increases in prices may distort this process and lead to inefficiency.

The price mechanism performs an important function by sending signals to consumers and firms.

The financial sector of the economy processes savings to create funds for firms and households to borrow. High inflation discourages saving: as prices rise, the value of a given amount of money falls. This erosion in the value of money makes saving unrewarding: £100 in a bank account will have a purchasing power of less than that amount one month or one year later. Even though interest rates tend to rise when inflation increases (the real rate of interest is calculated by subtracting the inflation rate from the nominal rate of interest) it is unlikely that they will rise sufficiently to outweigh high inflation rates. This leads to a negative real rate of interest. When this occurs, there is no real incentive for households to save. Instead, it is rational to borrow as much money as possible as, over time, the real value of that debt falls and becomes easier to repay.

Inflation also redistributes income from savers to borrowers. Households living on fixed incomes that are not index-linked (adjusted for the rate of inflation) will experience a decline in their real standard of living. Households with large debts will benefit, providing their incomes rise at least in part with inflation. Again, this can lead to short-termism in the economy and there may be a shortage of funds in capital markets.

Inflation can harm trade, particularly if UK inflation outstrips inflation in other countries. The prices of UK goods rise more quickly than those of its trading rivals and so demand for UK goods falls, both domestically (where imports become relatively cheaper, leading to import penetration) and abroad. This growing imbalance can lead to, or in the case of the UK, add to, the current account deficit.

There are other costs associated with high inflation. When prices are rising rapidly, it is important that firms increase (and publicise) their higher prices to consumers, otherwise profit margins will be quickly eroded by higher costs (the prices of raw materials). Thus 'menu costs' arise as firms must monitor and update their prices frequently.

In addition, consumers may shop around more during periods of rapid price increases. Some suppliers may increase their price more slowly than others, and thus there are search costs or 'shoe leather' costs of inflation. This covers the opportunity cost of the time spent looking for less expensive goods as well as transport, congestion and pollution costs to both consumers and society.

Stagflation is one possible outcome when high inflation occurs alongside high unemployment. This usually occurs when cost-push inflation combines with the low or even negative growth rates associated with recession. Examples include periods in the 1970s when major economies such as the UK and USA saw oil price rises feed into higher costs for firms at a time when growth was already fragile due to both cyclical factors (weak aggregate demand growth) and structural weaknesses on the supply-side of the policy (both economies were making painful transitions as the manufacturing sector declined and the service sector was yet to grow to take its place as the major employer in the economy).

The UK economy experienced rising inflation and unemployment during 2008 as cost-push pressures from high energy and clothing prices combined with a serious slowdown in economic growth.

The benefits of inflation?

It could be argued that some inflation is beneficial to the economy as it reduces the risk of deflation.

Deflation arises when there is a sustained fall in the general price level. This is sometimes confused with falling prices. In most economies, the price of some goods and services will fall over time. This is particularly true for the UK in recent years, where the prices of consumer durables such as cars and electronic goods have fallen. Falling prices may arise through increased availability of cheaper imports, increased efficiency of suppliers (both domestic and foreign) or changes in tariff or subsidy levels. It is rare, however, for the price index to fall. This is because households will react to the fall in the price of some goods by increasing demand for that good or for other goods. Thus the overall spending of the average household does not fall, and the CPI will still show some increase in the cost of living. Economists sometimes refer to this as benign deflation: decreases in the price of some goods due to supply-side growth.

Deflation can arise, but is usually a symptom of an economy in serious difficulties. Usually only a prolonged and deep recession could create the economic conditions necessary for the average spending of a typical household to actually fall. Economists call the result of such a decline in aggregate demand as malign deflation.

The UK has an inflation target of CPI of between 1% and 3%, in contrast to a Eurozone target of <2%. It could be argued that pursuing a lower inflation target will reduce the growth rate of the economy, thus increasing the risk of deflation.

In addition, the redistribution effects of inflation may help an economy suffering from high levels of debt, whether personal or household, corporate, or government. Inflation erodes the real value of liabilities as well as assets and providing households see incomes rise at least in line with the price index, the real burden of mortgage repayments will fall over time. Homeowners and debtors may therefore benefit from an inflation dividend, providing growth, jobs and price rises settle to a stable level and do not spiral out of control.

Inflation policy

Demand management measures such as monetary and fiscal policy can be used to control inflation in a similar way to unemployment. Demand pull inflation is more likely to arise during a boom in the economy and it is possible for the government and/or the central bank to intervene to slow aggregate demand growth to more suitable levels. The operation of these policy instruments is explored further in Chapters 7 and 8.

In addition, supply-side policy can play its part in establishing and maintaining low inflation. The supply-side of the economy is concerned with the efficiency of factors of production (land, labour, capital, enterprise) in supplying the goods and services demanded by households, firms and government. Chapter 9 will examine how supply-side policy can help achieve low inflation and other macroeconomic objectives.

Summary questions

1. What is inflation? How is it measured?

2. Explain, using a numerical example, what is meant by a negative real rate of interest.

3. How does inflation redistribute income from savers to borrowers?

4. What other problems can inflation cause for an economy?

5. "Deflation is a symptom rather than a cause of economic problems." To what extent is this true?

Extension questions

A. Why must economists adjust the contents of the basket of goods over time? Research recent examples of goods or services that have been weighted upwards or downwards in the UK CPI measure?

B. Which types of firms may be most affected by (a) menu costs and (b) search costs of inflation?

C. 'Demand management policy is unable to cure stagflation.' To what extent do you agree with this statement?

Chapter 5

The Balance of Payments and Exchange Rates

The current account

Exports are UK goods and services sold to households, firms or governments in other countries whereas imports are foreign goods and services sold to UK households, firms or government. The difference between the value of exports (X) and the value of imports (M) is the current account position on the balance of payments, usually shortened to the **current account**.

There are four components of the current account: **trade in goods**, **trade in services**, **investment income** and **transfers**. Each component covers both outflows (payments to foreigners, i.e. imports) and inflows (payments by foreigners, i.e. exports). The relative size of total exports versus total imports gives the current account position.

If X = M the current account is in balance.

If X > M there is a current account surplus.

If X < M there is a current account deficit.

The UK has experienced a prolonged current account deficit in recent years. Figure 5.1 shows the current account deficit in the UK from 1990 onwards.

Figure 5.1: UK current account, £bn

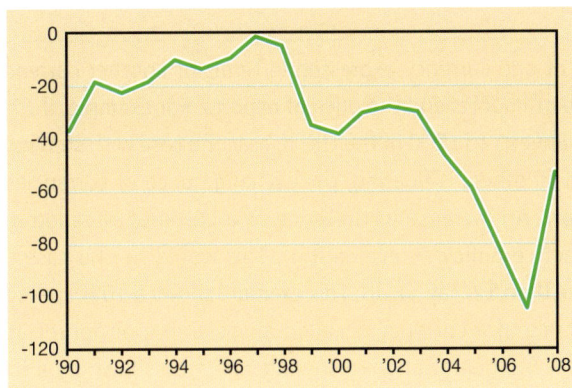

Source: ONS

The UK current account deficit

The four components of the current account help to illustrate how the deficit has arisen.

Figure 5.2 shows that the key factor contributing to current account deficit is the substantial (and increasing) deficit on trade in goods. Trade in services and investment income have both been in surplus over the period shown, showing that in both cases earnings from exports exceed payments for imports. For a service-sector economy such as the UK this is not surprising, and the large business and finance sector of the UK economy has contributed to surplus on investment income resulting from returns on UK business activity abroad.

Figure 5.2: UK current account by component, £bn

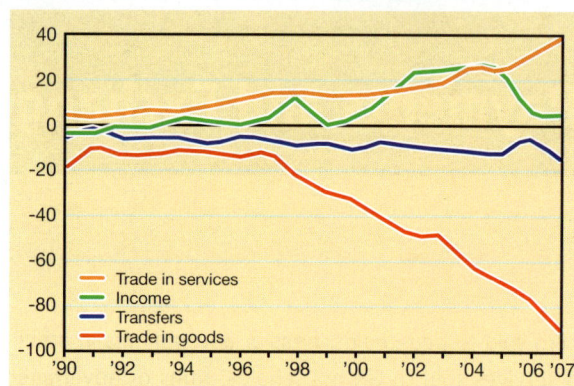

Source: www.hm-treasury.gov.uk

Transfers generally arise from the repatriation of earnings. The UK has a large number of migrant workers and earnings sent home contribute to the deficit on this component of the current account.

The UK has a large deficit on the trade in goods for several reasons. Firstly, the UK has, until recently, experienced strong and pro-longed economic growth since the early 1990s and as aggregate demand has grown, the higher level of spending has sucked in imports. In addition, as unemployment has fallen and the UK has approached full capacity, the ability of domestic suppliers to meet demand has reduced, thus imports have risen to meet the high level of demand. Firms have also had to import higher levels of raw materials and energy from abroad as production has risen, deepening the deficit further.

Secondly, fundamental shifts in the pattern of trade and business activity have increased world trade to unprecedented levels in recent years. Globalisation is not a new phenomenon but it has been a powerful force nonetheless. Greater openness to trade by countries such as China has resulted in low wage economies becoming large exporters of manufactured goods, leaving high wage-cost economies losing market share both at home and abroad.

Thirdly, sterling has been strong in recent years. When the exchange rate is high, UK producers lose competitiveness against foreign suppliers. The next section examines exchange rates in greater detail and considers their importance for the macroeconomy.

Exchange rates

An **exchange rate** is the price of one currency expressed in terms of another currency. Exchange rates have a direct impact on the price of imports and the price of exports. For example, if £1 = $2, a good with a sale price of $400 in the USA converts to £200 in the UK. If, as is the case with sterling (£), the exchange rates between one currency and all others is floating, the exchange price of currencies is free to change according to demand and supply. An increase in the price of a currency is called a strengthening or appreciation (or, if caused by active policy, a revaluation). This would be the case if, from the above example, £1 was now worth more than $2, say $2.20. This example shows a 10% appreciation in the value of sterling. A decrease in the price of a currency is called a weakening or depreciation (or, if caused by active policy, a devaluation). A 5% depreciation in sterling would be shown by a fall from £1 = $2 to £1 = $1.90.

When sterling is strong UK goods become more expensive abroad, and foreign goods are relatively cheaper. Thus there is a shift away from demand for UK-produced goods towards cheaper alternatives. This leads to a worsening of the current account position, as both X (the value of exports) falls and M (the value of imports) rises. Similarly, a weakening of sterling should see the demand for UK goods rise, increasing X, and a fall in imports as foreign goods become relatively more expensive, reducing M.

The FOREX market: trade, hot money and speculation

Changes in the exchange rate result from shifts in the FOREX, or foreign exchange market. This is where currencies are traded and the main determinant of demand and supply is trade in goods and services.

Figure 5.3: The foreign exchange market in equilibrium

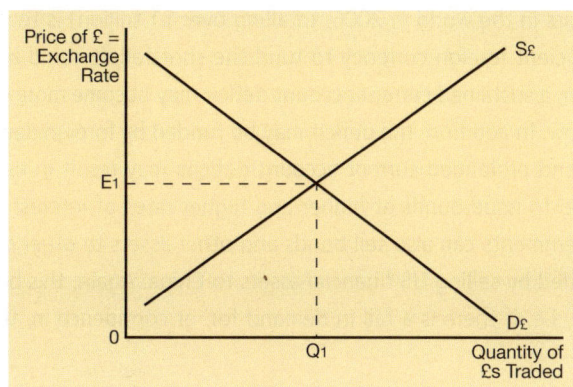

Figure 5.3 shows the demand for sterling (D£) and the supply of sterling (S£) and the equilibrium exchange rate, E1. However, in reality the supply of sterling is higher than demand, and this difference represents the current account deficit.

Figure 5.4: A current account deficit

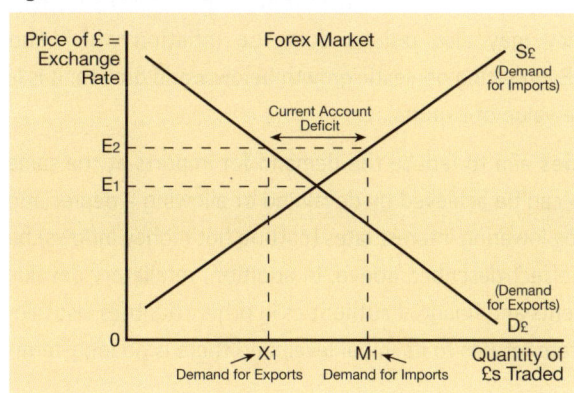

Figure 5.4 shows (M1-X1) as the current account deficit. Note that the excess supply of sterling is needed to buy the foreign currencies required to fund imports. A basic understanding of market theory would suggest that the exchange rate E2 is unsustainable in the long-run: the FOREX market should see the exchange rate fall until the market clears at E1. The factors preventing this from happening are threefold.

Firstly, hot money inflows help to keep sterling strong. Hot money is the name given to funds held by international investors who seek the highest (real) return. Each country has a different interest rate and inflation rate, and it is the real rate of interest that attracts hot money. Similarly, a lower real interest rate would cause hot money outflows. For the UK, interest rates at times have been higher than European alternatives and inflation has been low and stable in recent years, hence the attractiveness of sterling to investors.

Secondly, strong growth and a flexible commercial sector have attracted foreign direct investment (FDI) in recent years. This business spending in the UK has helped sustain the demand for sterling. Thirdly, speculation plays a large role in currency movements. Speculators are traders who gamble on short-run movements in a financial instrument such as a share or a currency. If the majority of speculators believe that a currency will fall they will sell the currency, and this increase in supply will put downward pressure on the price. A collective belief that a currency will strengthen will cause demand to rise, with a consequent increase in price. It can be seen that speculation can lead to a 'self-fulfilling prophecy' and for this reason exchange rates can be affected by both positive and negative speculative behaviour.

Is a current account deficit a problem?

The economic implications of a current account deficit are unclear. Shifts in demand and trade will cause temporary surpluses and deficits; economists begin to show an interest in a deficit when it persists into the long-run. There are also particular cases when a deficit may actually be desirable, for example when a developing country is importing new technologies to boost the long-run productive potential of the economy, or where a natural disaster has wiped out domestic harvests and infrastructure and both consumer and capital goods are being imported to restore and rebuild the standard of living. High oil prices may also cause current account imbalances as the high price benefits oil exporters but worsens the current account for oil importing nations.

The key issue surrounding current account deficits for countries such as the UK, Spain and the USA (the countries with the biggest deficits in the world in 2006, totalling over $1 trillion) is that of sustainability. Providing an economy has sufficient foreign currency to fund the shortfall, it could be argued that the deficit is not a problem. However, a sustained current account deficit may become more worrying if foreign currency reserves begin to run low. In addition, the deficit may be funded by foreign demand for domestic currency, shares and property, and prolonged current account deficits may result in rising debt levels as national governments are forced to issue bonds at higher and higher rates of interest to support global demand for their currency. Governments can also sell bonds and other assets to other countries; much of the US deficit with China is funded by selling US financial assets to China. Again, this becomes a problem when it becomes unsustainable, i.e. if there is a fall in demand for, or confidence in, the deficit nation's assets.

There are three possible responses to a current account deficit: expenditure-reducing, expenditure-switching and protectionism.

Expenditure-reducing policies aim to slow down economic growth, in turn reducing demand for imported goods. Such a policy may also reduce domestic inflation which should increase the competitiveness of UK exports. By lowering domestic growth below world growth, it is likely that the value of imports will fall relative to the value of exports.

Expenditure-switching policies aim to reduce the demand for imports at the same time as boosting demand for exports. This switch can be achieved by devaluing or allowing a depreciation of the domestic currency. This may by achieved by lowering interest rates (cutting hot money inflows) but this may conflict with the expenditure-reducing effect described above. In addition, retaliatory devaluations are possible (and likely), where the governments and financial authorities in other countries also allow their currency to depreciate. Thus the exchange rate returns to its initial level, and there is no long-term impact on exports relative to imports.

Protectionism is the attempt by a national government or trading group to reduce imports by increasing their price (through import taxes, or tariffs), restricting their quantity (quotas), or using bureaucracy to deter foreign sellers (trade restrictions, slow customs practices or high safety standards). The main problem with protectionism is also one of retaliation: most countries will respond by imposing similar policies on exports from protectors, and again if exports fall as well as imports, the overall impact on the current account is unclear.

Summary questions

1. What is meant by a current account deficit?
2. What factors may explain the persistent current account deficit in the UK in recent years?
3. What influences the exchange rate between two currencies?
4. How may an expenditure-reducing policy affect the current account position?
5. How may an expenditure-switching policy affect the current account position?

Extension questions

A. What factors limit the time period over which a current account deficit can persist?
B. Using examples, evaluate the success of protectionist policies in reducing imports into a country or a trading bloc.
C. 'A current account surplus must be more beneficial to the economy than a current account deficit.' To what extent do you agree with this statement?

Chapter 6

Aggregate Demand and Aggregate Supply

The relationships between economic growth, unemployment and inflation are at the heart of macro-economic analysis. The aggregate demand (AD) and aggregate supply (AS) model allows economists to show how shocks to the economy will affect these variables. An economic shock is an impact on demand or supply from inside (endogenous shocks) or outside (exogenous shocks) the economy. Increases in aggregate demand represent actual growth (increases in spending); increases in aggregate supply represent trend growth (increases in productive potential).

Aggregate demand (AD)

Aggregate Demand (AD) is total spending in the economy, or actual GDP. Spending is undertaken by households, firms, governments and foreigners. The formula for AD is:

AD = C + I + G + (X − M)

Where C = consumption (spending by households), I = investment (capital spending by firms), G = government spending and (X-M) is the value of exports minus the value of imports (net spending on UK goods by foreigners).

In the UK, typically (and very approximately) 60% of GDP is due to consumption, 20% investment, 25% government spending, with the extra compensated by a negative value on net exports (X-M) resulting from the current account deficit.

Figure 6.1: Aggregate demand

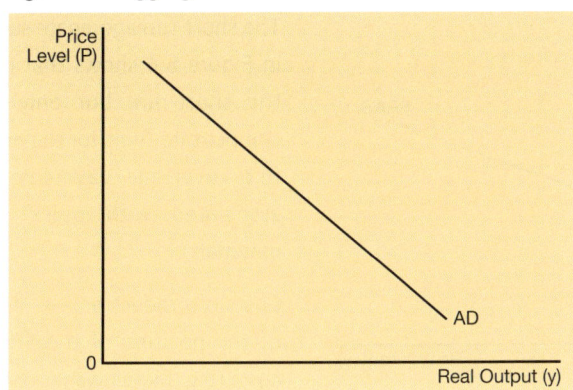

Figure 6.1 shows the relationship between AD, real output and the price level.

The aggregate demand curve shows that the price level and real output are negatively related. The AD curve will shift outwards (Figure 6.2) with any increase in C, I, G or (X-M), and shift inwards (Figure 6.3) with any fall in C, I, G or (X-M).

Consumption is determined by willingness and ability of households to buy goods and services. Higher incomes, lower interest rates, easy credit, greater wealth and strong confidence about the future will all all increase consumption.

Figure 6.2: An outward shift in aggregate demand

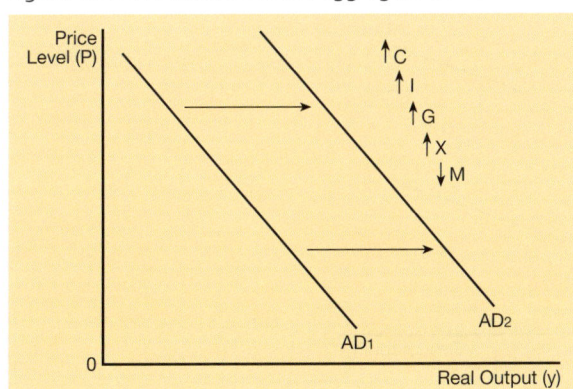

Investment is determined by the willingness and ability of firms to expand output. Strong demand and high business confidence and cheap factors of production encourage greater investment by firms, and low interest rates make borrowing funds cheaper and thus investment will rise.

Figure 6.3: An inward shift in aggregate demand

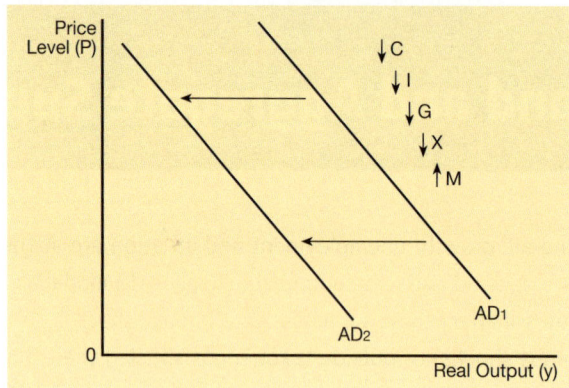

Government spending is determined by the strength of the economy and the objectives of government. This is covered in greater detail in Chapter 8.

Net exports (X-M) are determined by the demand for UK goods abroad and the demand for foreign goods in the UK. One important determinant is the exchange rate, which directly affects the price of exports and imports and is a key influence on the international competitiveness of a country's goods abroad.

Aggregate supply in the short-run

The aggregate supply curve shows the total output level of all firms in the economy at a given price level. The price (i.e. revenue per unit sold) acts as an incentive to firms: higher prices increase the willingness and ability of firms to supply the good or service.

The responsiveness of supply to changes in price differs from the short-run to the long-run. Economists use the short-run to describe a period in which at least one of the factors of production (land, labour, capital, enterprise) is fixed in quantity. For example, a car manufacturer can increase output quickly by paying labour to work overtime and/or increasing orders for more raw materials. But to increase the scale of production, for example to move to a larger factory, will not be possible until the long-run. Note that there is no definitive time placed on how long the long-run is: this will be a matter for each industry and the availability of suitable factors of production.

Figure 6.4: The short-run aggregate supply curve

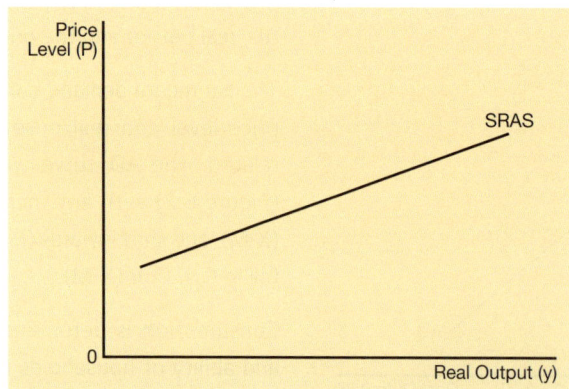

The short-run aggregate supply (SRAS) curve in Figure 6.4 shows that output can rise in the short-run, but only if prices rise to compensate firms for the extra costs involved (e.g. overtime payments or higher costs associated with quick delivery of raw materials).

Costs of production are the key determinant of the position of the SRAS curve. Higher costs (e.g. higher wages or higher commercial rents) will shift SRAS back whereas a fall in costs will shift SRAS to the right (see Figure 6.5).

Figure 6.5: A shift in the short-run aggregate supply curve

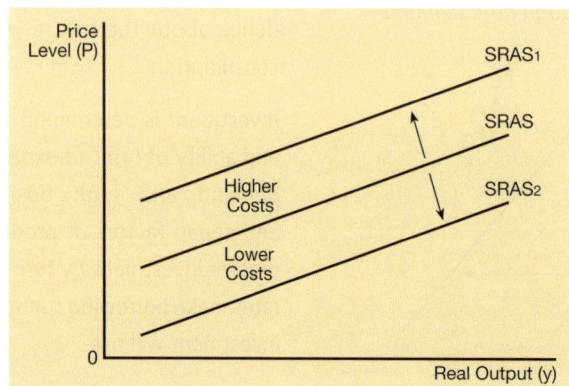

Aggregate supply in the long-run

The shape of the **Long-Run Aggregate Supply** (LRAS) curve is at the centre of a key debate in macroeconomics: put simply, can government intervention in the level of aggregate demand in the economy lead to long-run increases in the output level?

Figure 6.6: The Classical model

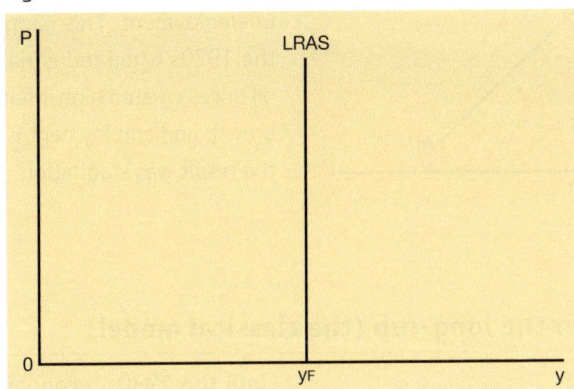

There are two main schools of thought: the Keynesian (or Neo-Keynesian) and the Classical (or Monetarist). For simplicity, these opinions on the LRAS curve will be referred to as Keynesian and Classical. The Classical school of economics stems mainly from the work of Adam Smith, who published The Wealth of Nations in 1776. The Classical model (Figure 6.6) assumes that the LRAS is vertical at the full employment level of national income (y_F).

Note that the LRAS, like the PPF, shows the productive potential of the economy. According to the Classical model the economy is always at full employment. The Keynesians, on the other hand, do not assume that the economy is always at full employment (Figure 6.7). Keynesians and their followers believe that it is possible that real output can fall below y_F, as in recessions such as the Great Depression of the 1930s. John Maynard Keynes wrote his seminal work, The General Theory of Employment, Interest and Money, in the 1930s when high levels of unemployment caused misery across the USA, Europe and the rest of the world.

Figure 6.7: The Keynesian model

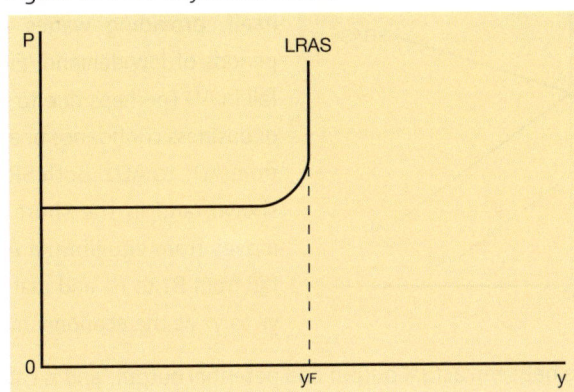

Macroeconomic equilibrium in the short-run

Macroeconomic equilibrium occurs where aggregate demand = aggregate supply, and therefore in the short-run where AD = SRAS.

Changes in the positions of the AD curve and SRAS curve will change the equilibrium price and real output levels.

Figure 6.8: A change in macroeconomic equilibrium

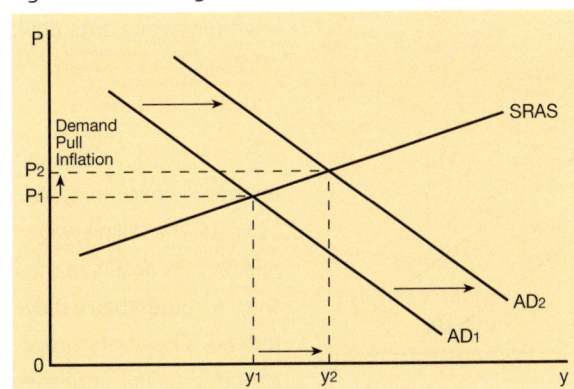

Figure 6.8 shows how rising AD may lead to higher real output, but at the expense of higher prices. These higher prices are called, in this instance, demand-pull inflation.

Figure 6.9 shows how higher prices can result from a fall in supply due to higher costs of production. Higher wages, oil prices or other costs will shift SRAS1 back to SRAS2 and this causes a fall in real output and rising prices, called cost-push inflation.

Figure 6.9: The impact of higher costs

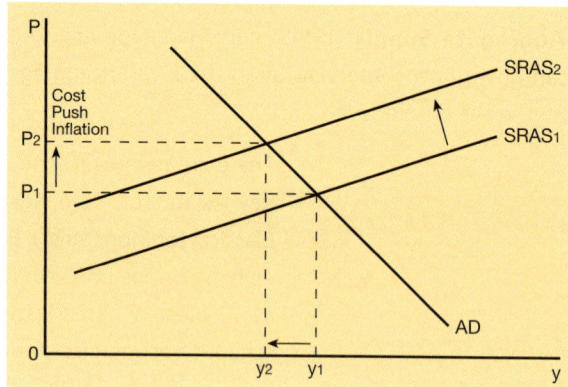

One problem associated with cost-push inflation is that of **stagflation**. As shown on Figure 6.9, the increase in prices from P1 to P2 is accompanied by a fall in real output from y1 to y2. Stagflation occurs when higher prices are accompanied by falling output and rising unemployment. This happened in the UK in the 1970s when industrial action and rising oil prices created high inflation at a time when growth and employment were already fragile: the result was stagflation.

Macroeconomic equilibrium in the long-run (the classical model)

Figure 6.10: A fall in real output

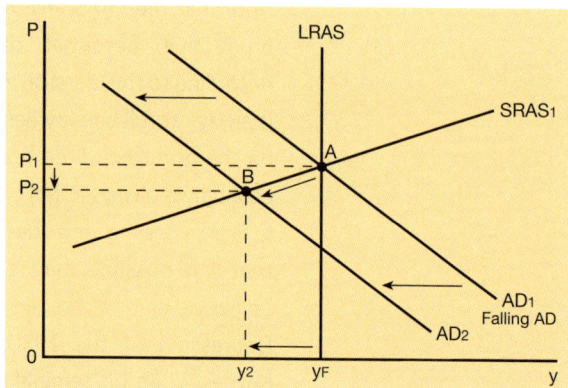

Until the 1930s, economists believed that unemployment (and therefore recession) was a short-run phenomenon which would cure itself, providing wages could fall during periods of low demand. Figure 6.10 shows a fall in AD (perhaps due to a loss of consumer or business confidence or a fall in investment) from AD1 to AD2. Both SRAS1 and LRAS are shown, and in the short-run the economy moves from equilibrium A to B, thus prices fall from P1 to P2 and real output falls below yF to y2 as the economy moves down SRAS1.

(yF-y2) represents the difference between actual output and potential output, and is called an output gap. This is actually a negative output gap, as the formula used is actual output minus potential output, also known as a recessionary or contractionary gap. Similarly, a positive output (or expansionary) gap occurs when actual output is above potential output.

As output is below the potential level in the short-run, there are unemployed resources in the economy. The most obvious (and damaging) factor to be unemployed is labour. Although empty fields and factories and unused machines represent a lost opportunity to the economy, they do not have wants, needs and desires and dependent families. Thus when economists refer to unemployment they are concerned primarily with unemployed labour. Microeconomics tells us that when there is an excess supply of a good this will result in a fall in equilibrium price. Classicists assume that labour behaves in a similar way: unemployment puts downward pressure on prices as firms can lower wages for both new and existing workers.

Figure 6.11: The impact of falling wages

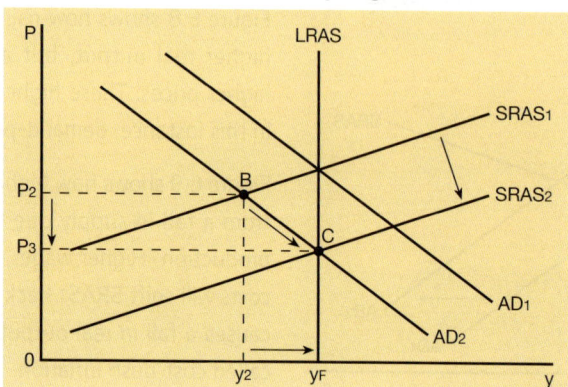

Figure 6.11 shows the impact of lower wages on the macroeconomy. As SRAS is determined by costs, the falling wages shift SRAS1 out to SRAS2. This occurs in the long-run: there is a shift in, rather than a movement along, SRAS. Indeed, Classicists propose that wages will continue to fall until there is no longer any

Figure 6.12: The impact of rising wages

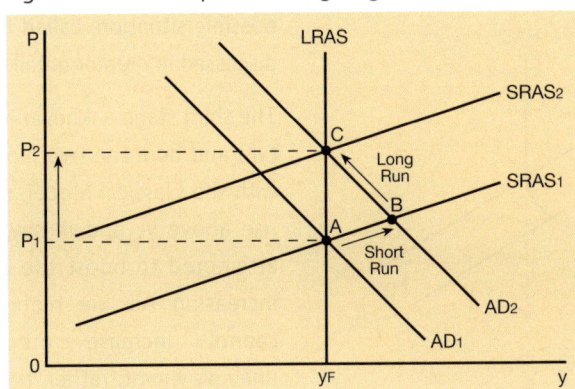

unemployment in the economy and there is a return to full employment at y$_F$, this time at equilibrium C. The fall in AD and prices is fully compensated by the fall in wages. Economists say that, at this point, real wages return to the same position as at equilibrium A.

Similarly, an increase in AD at full employment can increase output further, but only in the short-run. This positive output gap cannot be sustained in the long-run as the shortage of workers will push up wages, pushing SRAS to the left and returning the economy to the full employment level of national income, y$_F$, but at a higher price level of p$_2$. This is shown in Figure 6.12

LRAS: The Keynesian model

The experience of economies in the 1930s led John Maynard Keynes to challenge the assumption that wages will fall in the long-run to absorb unemployed workers. Keynes' most famous quote is 'In the long-run we're all dead', and his work focused on the possibilities for government intervention to reduce unemployment – and its harmful impacts on the economy and society.

Figure 6.13: The Keynesian LRAS

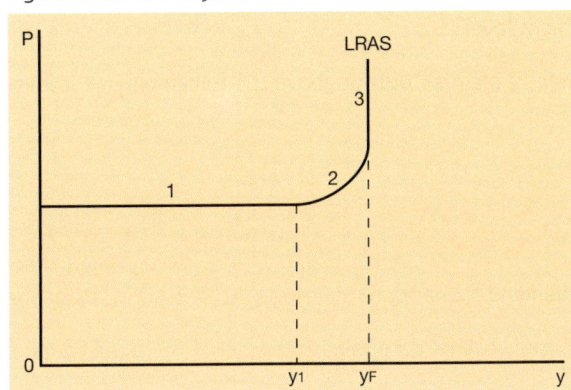

Figure 6.10 above showed how falling AD can open an output gap and cause unemployment. Classicists believe that wages will adjust downwards, but Keynes argued that this may not be the case. Workers still in employment may enjoy protection, such as long-term contracts or a powerful trade union, or employers may choose to employ fewer workers at the same wage rather than more workers at lower wages. In this case, wages are said to be sticky downwards and unemployment may persist into the long-run.

The Keynesian LRAS is shown in Figure 6.13 and has three stages.

The first stage of the Keynesian LRAS is called mass unemployment and occurs between real output levels 0 and y$_1$. Over this output range firms are willing and able to increase output without requiring an increase in prices. Such a position is likely in a recession.

The second stage shows a trade-off. Real output can rise above y$_1$ but higher output (and consequently lower unemployment) can only occur alongside upward pressure on prices, i.e. inflation.

During the first and second stages of Keynesian LRAS there is scope for the government to intervene in the macroeconomy to create jobs. As AD = C + I + G + (X-M), if AD has fallen due to lower consumption (C) or investment (I), higher government spending (G) can make up this shortfall. AD can be returned to its original level of AD$_1$ via higher government spending and/or lower

Mass unemployment is the first stage of the model.

Figure 6.14: Fiscal expansion

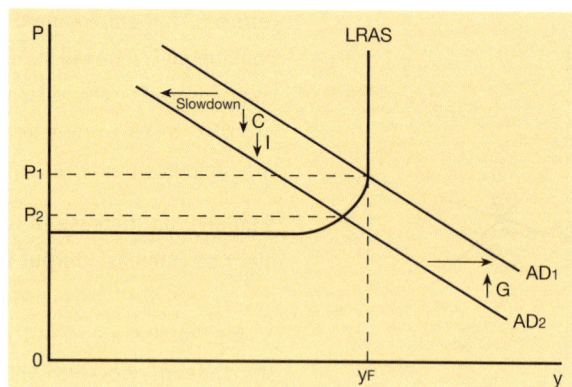

taxes. This is shown in Figure 6.14. This possible situation, called fiscal expansion, is discussed in greater detail in Chapter 8.

The third stage is known as full employment (y_F) and here the two models converge. As with the Classical Model, real output cannot rise above y_F and if, say, the government attempted to boost the economy through increasing AD via higher spending they cannot increase output or reduce unemployment; rather, they will only create inflation.

Using the AS/AD model: a summary

The AS/AD model is a powerful tool of macroeconomic analysis. The model links output (and therefore growth), employment (and therefore unemployment) and prices (and therefore inflation). Changes in the macroeconomy can be explained as a shift outwards or inwards in either aggregate demand or aggregate supply, and the impact of the resulting shift in equilibrium levels of prices and output can be read on the axes. Depending on the shape of LRAS, changes in AD can be used to reduce unemployment by creating short-run growth, or economic recovery.

In the Keynesian model this is possible but only when there is spare capacity in the economy, i.e. actual output is below the full employment level.

In the Classical model it is possible to increase output above the full employment level in the short-run – but not in the long-run.

Summary questions

1. What is meant by aggregate demand? What determines the level of AD in the economy?

2. What is meant by aggregate supply? What determines the level of AS in the economy?

3. Why does SRAS have a positive gradient?

4. Explain how both higher government spending and lower taxes will increase AD.

5. Using both the Classical and Keynesian models, show the short-run and long-run impact on inflation and unemployment of an increase in AD.

Extension questions

A. If LRAS represents productive potential, is it ever possible for a positive output gap to occur? How?

B. 'Real wages determine employment levels.' Explore why this may be true from the point of view of workers and firms?

C. Why may macroeconomists find it difficult to empirically test whether wages are 'sticky downwards'?

Chapter 7

Monetary Policy

An introduction to banking

Banks provide households and firms with the means to save. When savings are deposited, the bank may then lend some or all of those funds to other households or firms. Thus savings (a withdrawal from the circular flow of income) are used to fund investment (an injection). The central bank (in the UK, the Bank of England) oversees the banking sector. High street (or 'commercial') banks such as HSBC and Natwest have accounts with the Bank of England. Among other functions, the Bank of England regulates the banking sector and is responsible for issuing currency (notes and coins) to the economy. The Bank of England is also responsible for monetary policy in the UK.

The Monetary Policy Committee

New Labour were elected to government on 1st May 1997 and on 6th May the Bank of England was granted operational responsibility to set the base rate of interest. The Monetary Policy Committee (MPC) of the Bank of England is responsible for achieving the target level of inflation, currently CPI between 1% and 3%.

Monetary Policy is currently synonymous with interest rate policy in the UK. In the past, governments have attempted to use other monetary measures to control the macroeconomy, including controlling the money supply (e.g. the Thatcher government's Monetarist experiment in the 1990s). The money supply can be measured in several ways, from the notes and coins in circulation (narrow money) to more inclusive measures which include bank accounts (near money) and the availability of credit (broad money). The larger the money supply, the greater the risk of inflation. This may be exacerbated by printing money: allowing the money supply to increase, e.g. to cope with debt crises. Other possible policies involve setting reserve ratio requirements which set a limit on the ratio of saving deposits banks can lend back to households and firms. A higher reserve asset ratio decreases the potential money supply in the economy.

Globalisation has made capital markets much more difficult to control by individual governments and central banks. A household or firm wishing to borrow money to fund spending or investment can borrow from overseas as well as from domestic banks. For this reason, many central banks have switched monetary control away from controlling the money supply towards controlling the cost of money, i.e. interest rates.

In October 2008 the MPC cut the base rate of interest by 0.50% despite CPI inflation of over 5%. This was on the stated belief that inflationary pressure was likely to subside dramatically in 2009 as the UK economy entered recession, and thus this cut in base rate illustrates the long time lag associated with this policy instrument.

The Monetary Policy transmission mechanism

The MPC sets the base rate and this influences all interest rates in the economy (the rates paid by borrowers and the rates paid to savers by commercial banks), and these in turn affect the level of aggregate demand, and therefore the price level and inflation. The base rate is the interest charged by the Bank of England to commercial banks. Thus an increase in the base rate should, in the long-run, be passed on to savers and borrowers in the form of higher saving and borrowing rates.

This process of influence is called the **monetary policy transmission mechanism**: how changes in the base rate influence spending decisions by households and firms, and how these changes feed through to affect macroeconomic variables.

Households earn income by supplying labour to firms or from government benefits. Disposable income is the term used for income after income tax deductions and households can either spend this income or save it. Interest rates play an important function in influencing this decision.

The interest rate is both the cost of borrowing and the opportunity cost of spending. An increase in interest rates will particularly affect households with large debt levels (e.g. mortgages) as the cost of repaying their debt will rise. Households with high savings will benefit from rising interest rates and will have a stronger incentive to keep money in the bank rather than spending it.

Similarly, firms have debts and (perhaps) funds they are saving for possible investment opportunities. An increase in interest rates will make them less inclined to invest: if they need to borrow to do so, the higher rate of interest makes this more expensive to do; if they are using existing funds, the investment project will need to earn a higher return (this is sometimes called the 'hurdle rate') than the interest rate available from banks to make it worthwhile. The higher the interest rate, the fewer such profitable projects will be available. This relationship between investment and the interest rate is known as the marginal efficiency of capital (MEC) and is shown on Figure 7.1.

Figure 7.1: The marginal efficiency of capital curve

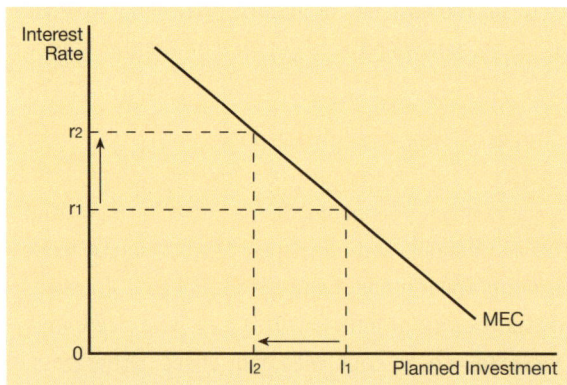

An increase in the base rate therefore reduces both consumption and investment. As these are both components of aggregate demand, this falls when the base rate rises. Figure 7.2 shows the impact of an increase in the base rate on AD, with subsequent fall in real output and prices.

Increasing the base rate is known as a contractionary monetary policy: it slows down economic growth and may be used to reduce inflation. On Figure 7.2 the shift from AD_1 to AD_2 leads to lower output and a fall in the price level. Such a policy can be used when the economy is overheating and demand-pull inflationary pressures are strong.

Figure 7.2: The impact of lower investment on aggregate demand

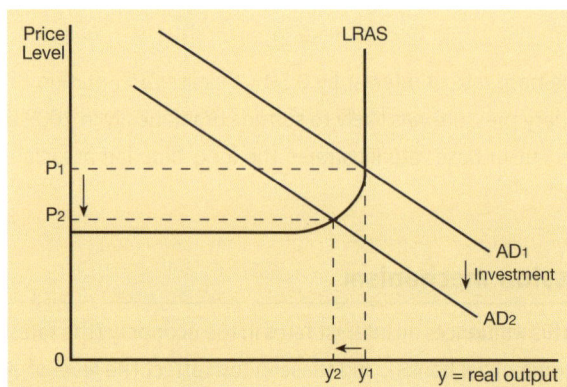

An expansionary monetary policy can be used to increase aggregate demand. Lower interest rates stimulate both higher consumption and higher investment which in turn increase AD and boost output and job creation. One consequence of higher output and falling unemployment is the risk of higher inflation. Such a policy will therefore only be used when inflation is low.

Thus monetary policy is a demand management policy as it shifts the position of the AD curve to influence price and output levels. The relationship between the base rate and economic activity is negative: higher base rates slow down economic growth and lower base rates speed up economic growth.

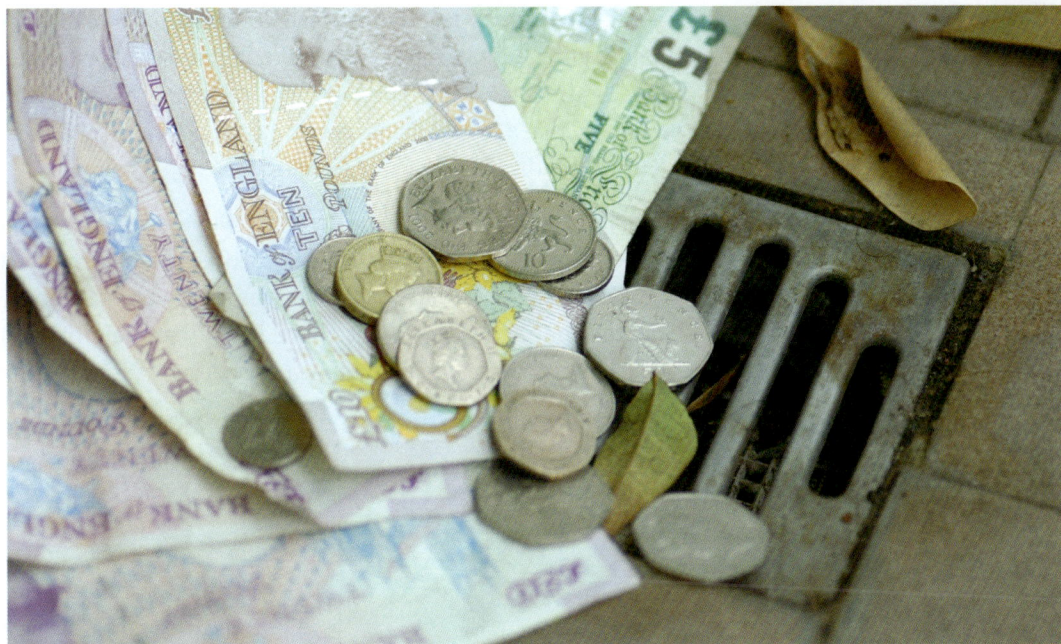

Monetary policy is quick to adapt to changes in the economic situation.

Advantages of using monetary policy to control the economy

1. Base rates are set each month by the MPC, using all available economic data to choose an appropriate rate to achieve the target level of CPI (2% plus or minus 1%). Thus monetary policy is quick to adapt to changes in the economic situation.

2. Most households and firms have savings and/or debt, and so a change in the base rate will have a direct impact on most economic agents.

3. Confidence is an important factor in the macroeconomy. Consumer confidence and business confidence determine the future expectations of households and firms respectively. An increase in the base rate will not only reduce post-debt repayment income, it will also send a signal to the economy that prices are rising too rapidly, and thus future increases in interest rates may be likely. This may reduce confidence and help to slow down growth in consumption and investment.

4. Since 1997 in the UK, the independence of the Bank of England has been seen as an effective means of limiting the government's ability to use spending to grow the economy too quickly. An expansionary fiscal policy would create inflationary pressure in the economy and would lead the MPC to raise base rates. Thus independent monetary policy can be an effective check on excessive government spending.

5. The role of expectations is crucial in determining inflation. If workers believe that prices will rise in the months ahead, they will demand large pay increases which, in turn, increase cost-push pressures in the economy. Expectations of low inflation were therefore created by giving a clear mandate to an independent central bank to specifically control inflation.

Disadvantages of using monetary policy to control the economy

1. The main criticism of using the base rate as a policy instrument is its *asymmetric impact*. Households with high levels of debt (e.g. families with large mortgages) are most adversely affected by higher interest rates. Similarly, households with large savings will benefit the most from higher interest rates as the yield on their funds increases. In addition, some saving and debt has fixed rates of interest, and yields and repayments in these cases will not change even if the base rate shifts significantly. This weakens, or at least delays, the monetary policy transmission mechanism.

2. Changes in the base rate take time to feed through the economy: the monetary policy transmission policy is slow and *time lags* occur. High street banks may not change their interest rates to customers immediately, and thus households and firms take time to adjust to changes in their financial circumstances. It is estimated that a change in the base rate takes between 6 and 12 months to influence GDP, and a further 6 to 12 months to fully impact on prices.

3. When there are significant time lags there is a greater possibility of inappropriate policy decisions. In effect, the MPC has to estimate the state of the economy between 1 and 2 years into the future. The base rate might be raised at a time when the economy appears to be growing strongly, but it may be the case that by the time the contractionary impact of the higher base rate bites, the economy is in slowdown and the higher interest rates may push growth down, even causing recession.

Figure 7.3: Bank of England's base rate

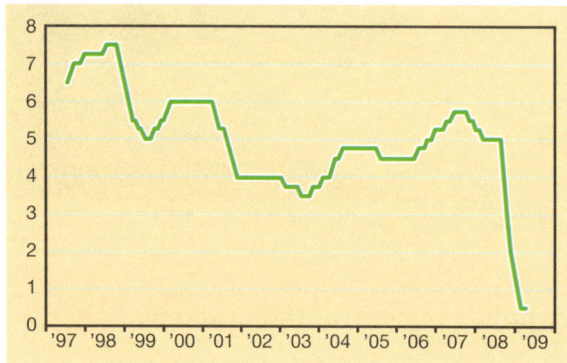

Source: Bank of England

4. The MPC tends to change base rates by 0.25% at a time. Figure 7.3 shows base rates in the UK since 2003.

Some economists argue that small changes in the base rate are not particularly effective, especially given the asymmetric impacts and long time lags involved. An increase in the base rate of 0.25% increases the mortgage payments of a household by about £20 per £100,000 borrowed; it could be argued that a fall in post-debt income of this amount is not likely to have a major impact on household spending.

The UK base rate was cut aggressively throughout late 2008 and early 2009 in an attempt to counter the deflationary problems created by the credit crisis in global financial markets. This topic is covered in greater depth in Chapter 10.

The Monetary Policy Committee at the Bank of England cut base rates aggressively from late 2008 to early 2009.

5. Interest rates influence the economy in both the short run and long run. A fall in interest rates will increase both aggregate demand (by stimulating increases in both consumption and investment) and aggregate supply, as firms increase investment in new technologies, infrastructure and worker training, thus increasing the future potential productive capacity of the economy. Conversely, higher interest rates will reduce the long run potential of the economy, and thus hinder economic performance in the future. A strict anti-inflation policy may therefore hold back the long-run prospects for economic growth.

Summary questions

1. Explain how interest rates affect the behaviour of both savers and borrowers.

2. What is the key factor the MPC takes into account when setting the base rate of interest?

3. Explain how a fall in the base rate affects the behaviour of households and firms in both the short-run and long-run.

4. What is the key advantage of an independent Bank of England?

5. What are the main drawbacks of using the base rate to control inflation?

Extension questions

A. As interest rates help to determine exchange rates, how may an increase in the base rate affect the current account position?

B. "Monetary policy affects different households and firms to different extents ; this makes current UK interest rate policy unfair." To what extent do you agree with this statement?

C. "The Credit Crisis has shown the increased impotence of base rate policy in an increasingly globalised world." To what extent do you agree with this statement?

Chapter 8

Fiscal Policy

Fiscal policy is the use of government spending and taxation to control the macroeconomy. The size of government spending (G) relative to tax revenue (T) is called the budget position. The budget (plans for government spending and tax collection) is set annually in the UK.

In a given year,

If G > T there is a budget deficit

If G = T there is a balanced budget

If G < T there is a budget surplus

Fiscal policy can affect both aggregate demand and aggregate supply, but it is used primarily in the UK as a demand-management tool, supplementing monetary policy to control the spending of households and firms.

Fiscal policy since 1997

When New Labour came to power in 1997 they were keen to dispel the view that Labour governments were less than careful with the public finances. Gordon Brown was keen to be seen as 'prudent and cautious' and to avoid running successive, large budget deficits to fund high levels of government-led expansion and high pay awards for public sector workers. In fact, up to 2000 the government maintained the spending plans set out by their Conservative predecessors.

Gordon Brown set two fiscal rules to control the government's finances. They are called the **Golden Rule** and the **Sustainable Investment Rule**.

Government spending can be divided into two groups: *capital spending* and *current spending*. Capital spending increases the productive capacity of the economy and thus shifts the PPF and LRAS to the right. Examples of capital spending are investment in infrastructure such as roads, airports and railways and building more hospitals and state schools. Current spending funds the day-to-day running of the public sector through purchases of raw materials (drugs for hospitals, school supplies) and paying wages (salaries to doctors, nurses, civil servants etc).

The Golden Rule states that *the budget should be balanced over an economic cycle*. As the economy moves from boom to downturn and possibly recession, government spending automatically increases and tax revenue falls. This is called fiscal drag and it has an automatic stabilising effect on the macroeconomy: as unemployment rises in a downturn, the budget automatically moves into deficit as the injection provided by government spending outweighs the withdrawal through taxes. This creates a net injection and aggregate demand rises (arrow B on Figure 8.1).

Similarly, as actual growth outstrips trend growth there is likely to be an increase in tax receipts (taxes are generally paid on income, spending and wealth, and all three of these tend to rise in a boom) and a possible fall in government spending as the number of households requiring benefits falls. This is called a fiscal dividend: the benefit to the budget position of strong short-run growth. But the net withdrawal slows the circular flow of income and may have a slight dampening impact on growth (arrow A).

Figure 8.1: Balancing the economy over the cycle

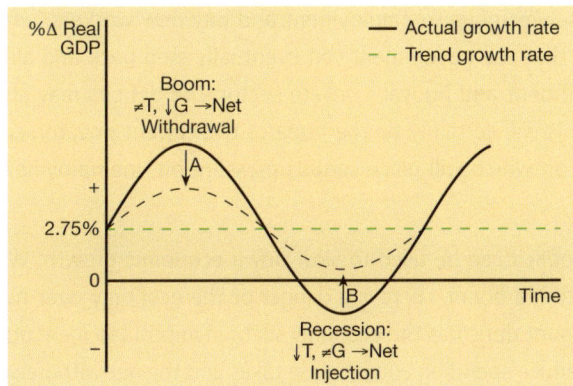

It is therefore unrealistic for the government to balance their budget every year: the pressures created by fluctuating growth levels would make spending and tax plans very difficult to maintain. But because some government spending – capital spending – is important in driving long-run growth, the Golden Rule does allow for an overall deficit over the cycle, providing any additional spending results from capital rather than current expenditure. It may be more accurate,

therefore, to state the Golden Rule as *current spending must equal tax receipts over the economic cycle*.

Budget deficits can be funded through excess tax receipts from previous surpluses or from borrowing. Governments borrow by issuing bonds. Bonds are a form of IOU: a promise to pay a certain amount of money at a certain point in the future. Bonds are sold to households and firms at home and abroad (they are a form of saving) and the funds raised can be used for capital spending projects (according to the fiscal rules) or to fund current expenditure (although such a situation may be unsustainable). Government bonds are sometimes called gilt-edged bonds, or gilts, as in theory they are backed by the government's reserves of gold. The total value of outstanding bonds at any given time is called the National Debt, and the Sustainable Investment Rule sets the National Debt at a maximum of 40% of GDP.

Thus the Golden Rule can be seen as a limit on current spending and the Sustainable Investment Rule as a limit on capital spending.

The fiscal rules in practice

The recession of 2009 led to the effective abandonment of the UK government's fiscal rules. Economic contraction dented official growth predictions and as a result tax revenues fell relative to increases in government spending. In addition, the Treasury committed to fiscal injections into the banking sector (including the part-nationalisation of some troubled banks) to attempt to restore savers' confidence.

Active fiscal policy

Figure 8.1 above shows the net injections and net withdrawals which arise as actual growth fluctuates around trend growth. In theory, this limits the severity of both booms and recessions by adjusting the level of actual growth towards the trend position in both cases. However, on top of these automatic stabiliser effects, it is possible for the government to actively manage aggregate demand through fiscal policy. This is called discretionary or active fiscal policy.

Keynesian economists support active fiscal policy to change the level of aggregate demand, especially during a recession. The Great Depression saw low levels of consumption and investment across the world and Keynes proposed that governments, in these circumstances, should run large budget deficits to generate a net injection into the circular flow of income.

Aggregate Demand (AD) = C + I + G + (X – M)

The shortfall in (C + I) can be overcome by high G (and low T). Put simply, the government generates demand when households and firms are unable or unwilling to buy goods and services themselves. Deficit spending is a form of expansionary fiscal policy and may take the form of public works, such as building roads or hospitals. The initial injection of funds creates jobs and the workers employed will spend their

higher incomes and this, in theory, leads to a multiplier effect where other firms benefit from the resulting increase in demand and themselves increase employment and pay new workers, who in turn increase spending… It may be possible that the government can eventually step back and allow further growth to be generated by a more confident and buoyant private sector; the deficits may also be repaid using the resulting fiscal dividend! This will certainly be the hope of the current government as the economy potentially faces a long recession which will place serious pressure on unemployment and the budget position.

Similarly, contractionary fiscal policy can be used to slow down economic growth. When actual output outstrips trend growth, e.g. during a boom, there is a danger of the economy over-heating, with higher inflation and a large current account deficit as the economy sucks in imports to meet domestic demand. In this case, the government will reduce spending and increase taxes and the net withdrawal from the circular flow should put downward pressure on consumption and investment growth – supported this time by a downward multiplier effect.

From the 1930s until the 1970s Keynesian-style demand management was popular in most economies. However, the problems associated with fiscal policy (and monetary policy – several of the problems outlined below are criticisms of demand-management policy in general) became more pronounced during the economic instability experienced in the 1970s.

Criticisms of fiscal policy

1. Crowding-out

Some economists argue that higher government spending will lead to lower investment. The theory argues that the more active role the government takes in supplying goods and services themselves, the fewer opportunities there will be for private entrepreneurs. Crowding-out can also be explained through impacts on the bond market and interest rates. A budget deficit may be funded by issuing bonds, but this absorbs spending by households and firms, thus reducing spending on non-bond goods and services: hence there is no overall increase in aggregate demand. Persuading households and firms to buy bonds may also require an increase in the interest rate offered. This places upward pressure on all interest rates in the economy, resulting in monetary contraction. Note that this negative effect will be weakened if the bonds are sold to foreigners as well as to UK households and firms.

2. Time lags

It takes time for fiscal policy to work. There are identification lags (seeing there is a problem), implementation lags (setting an appropriate policy to counter the problem) and impact lags (waiting for changes in taxes and spending levels to affect aggregate demand, and for this to influence price and employment levels). The UK budget is set once a year, limiting the scope for rapid responses to changes in the economic situation. Time lags are an example of government failure and, as with monetary policy, a possible scenario could be where the state of the macroeconomy changes significantly (for example, a sudden downturn in growth resulting from a shock to the domestic or even global economy) making the policy the opposite of that required (in this case, a previous boom has led to fiscal contraction which, by the time it takes effect, pushes the economy deeper into recession).

3. The shape of LRAS: the Classical Model

According to the Classical Model, any attempt by the government to increase output and reduce unemployment using aggregate demand policy will only create inflation in the long-run.

4. The position of AD on LRAS: the Keynesian Model

The success of demand-management policy (whether fiscal, monetary or both) depends on the existing level of unemployment, or spare capacity, in the economy. The nearer the economy is to full employment,

Figure 8.2: Aggregate demand and inflation

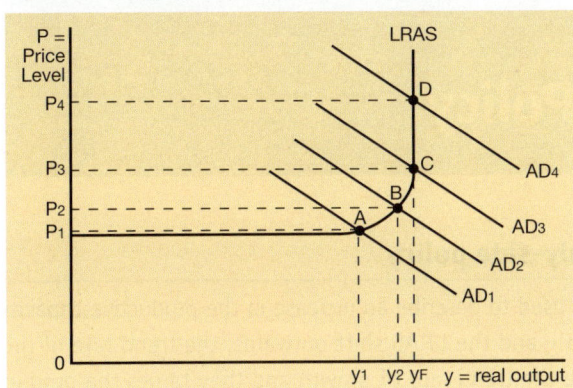

the more difficult it is for jobs to be created, and the higher the impact on prices and therefore inflation. As shown in Figure 8.2 the increase in aggregate demand from AD_1 to AD_2, AD_3 and AD_4 has successively lower impacts on real output (and therefore job creation) and involves higher and higher inflation.

Long-run implications of fiscal policy

Government expenditure increases aggregate demand but can also (if funding capital spending) increase long-run aggregate supply. Higher spending on healthcare, education and transport infrastructure leads to a healthier, more highly skilled workforce which wastes less time in traffic jams or on delayed trains. Taxes also have an important impact on the macroeconomy through the disincentives they create.

Income tax deters people from working. In theory, higher rates of income tax make it more likely that lower income households are better off on benefits (once working hours versus leisure time is taken into account) and that higher skilled and higher income workers look abroad for higher post-tax incomes under less punitive tax regimes ('brain drain').

Similarly, taxes on company profits (corporation tax) acts as a disincentive to entrepreneurship. Lower corporation tax encourage entrepreneurs to take greater risks as the post-tax reward for starting or expanding their firms is higher. Competitive tax regimes can also be used to attract investment and entrepreneurs from abroad.

Summary questions

1. What is the link between government spending, taxation and the budget position?
2. Distinguish between active fiscal policy and automatic stabilisers.
3. What is the link between the National Debt and a budget deficit? What happens to National Debt, in theory, if the government runs a budget surplus?
4. How does the LRAS curve influence the effectiveness of fiscal policy in determining the level of employment and unemployment in the economy?
5. How do taxes affect incentives in the economy?

Extension questions

A. What might happen to the macroeconomy if a government attempted to balance the budget each year rather than over an economic cycle?
B. 'Issuing bonds to finance current expenditure is unsustainable.' To what extent do you agree with this statement?
C. 'Higher rates of income tax make it more likely that lower income households are better off on benefits (once working hours versus leisure time is taken into account).' What is the price of one hour of your leisure time? How might you calculate this? How does this differ from the price of one hour of your teacher's time... or one hour of a banker's time?

Chapter 9

Supply-Side Policy

Supply-side growth and supply-side policy

Supply-side growth is the term used to describe an increase in the productive capacity of the economy. This is the rate at which the PPF and the LRAS shift outwards: the trend rate of growth. Supply-side policies aim to actively manage the trend rate of growth and they target the productivity (output per input) of factors of production, primarily labour productivity.

Supply-side growth may arise with or without government intervention. Advances in agriculture may increase the amount of farmable land and improve production, the population may expand as birth rates rise and life expectancy extends, inventors may develop new machines, and entrepreneurs may explore more effective business structures; these developments will increase the land, labour, capital and enterprise available.

In addition, the government may be able to boost supply-side growth through, say, land reclamation programmes, education policies, tax breaks for capital investment and improved management training.

Productivity

Productivity is a key measure of the performance of the supply-side of the economy. Put simply, an economy aims to convert factors of production (inputs) into the goods and services (output) demanded by households, firms and government. A highly productive economy will produce goods and services that are high in both quantity and quality, relative to the quantity and quality of inputs.

Supply-side policy and macroeconomic performance

Supply-side growth offers economists the 'holy grail' of non-inflationary growth. An increase in aggregate demand means more spending in the economy and this can increase employment and boost the government's finances through higher tax revenues, but this usually comes at the expense of greater inflationary pressure and, possibly, a worsening of the current account as the economy sucks in more imports.

Figure 9.1: Supply-side policies

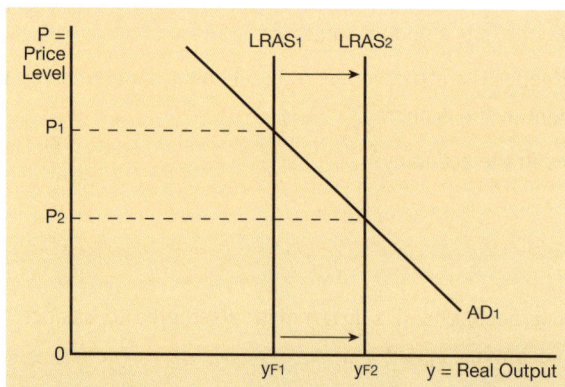

Supply-side growth also increases employment and tax revenues, but because output rises in line with demand (there is a movement along AD rather than a shift outwards – see Figure 9.1) there is no inflationary pressure. Indeed, prices may actually fall as the economy is now able to produce goods and services more efficiently. An additional bonus is that the current account may not deteriorate either; in fact the opposite may be the case: higher output meets both domestic and global demand, reducing the need to buy imports and possibly growing UK sales of exports to foreigners.

Supply-side policies in the UK since 1997

Supply-side policies are a powerful solution when applied to the conflicting objectives of low inflation and low unemployment. As shown above, increases in productive capacity can reduce unemployment and price

The government has targeted education as well as healthcare as ways of improving labour productivity.

inflation simultaneously. The current government has targeted education and healthcare as ways of improving labour productivity. A more highly skilled, educated and healthy workforce is able to work more effectively with fewer working days missed due to illness. In addition, a workforce with 'transferable skills' (literacy, numeracy, ICT) can adapt to changes in global demand and are less likely to be left with redundant skills and experience, thus reducing structural unemployment in the economy.

The UK labour force has seen changes in some key participation rates (the proportion of certain types of people choosing to work, rather than not work) in recent years. Firstly, the number of working mothers has risen. The government can make it easier for women to return to work after childbirth through legal protection and promoting part-time or flexible working arrangements. Educated and experienced women may otherwise leave the workforce either permanently (taking valuable skills and experience with them) or return to work in lower skill roles; both situations involve a decline in the human capital of the workforce – and therefore the economy.

In addition, older workers have been given better rights to prevent firms enforcing retirement ages which may not suit them. Again, valuable skills and experience can be retained, even if workers who have taken early retirement work part-time to supplement retirement pensions. The UK has also seen a rise in migrant workers, particularly from the accession countries of the EU such as Poland. During periods of strong economic growth it is usual to see gaps in the labour market: shortages of lower-skill workers who are willing to accept low wage employment. These gaps, particularly in urban centres and low-wage industries such as agricultural labouring, factories and hospitality work, have been filled to a large extent by workers coming to the UK from other countries.

Since 1997, the government has also introduced 'welfare-to-work' measures such as the tax credit system which aims to move people from welfare benefits to earned income. Although criticised by some as overly bureaucratic, the Institute for Fiscal Studies estimates that these measures have helped 50,000 single mothers move into part-time employment.

It should be said that developments such as those mentioned above are not greeted with universal popularity – not least, in some cases, by those most directly affected! Working parents may argue that it is the high cost of living, and high house prices in particular, which forces them both to return to work after parenthood. Similarly, older workers may blame the collapse of pension funds as the reason for continued participation in the workforce. The debate over the economic impact of immigration is

contentious and is too complex to be discussed here. Nonetheless, the supply of labour increases in all these cases, pushing out the PPF and the LRAS in the process – and, ceteris paribus, allowing non-inflationary growth to occur.

Other supply-side policies

Regional policy is used by the EU to boost local GDP in areas struggling with high levels of structural unemployment. Because traditional industries such as car manufacturing, mining and agriculture tend to be concentrated in certain geographic areas, when the industry declines or disappears altogether, the area can face severe economic hardship. Typical regional policies include investment in infrastructure and tax breaks or subsides to firms willing to move there.

Broadly speaking, any policy which aims to increase the incentive for producers to increase the quantity and/or quality of the goods is a supply-side policy.

In 1986 the Conservative government deregulated the UK financial system in what was known as the 'Big Bang'. In addition to increasing the opportunities for bankers, stock brokers and traders to earn higher salaries, this also increased the financial capital available to firms to invest. The success of the City of London still benefits UK business by creating more jobs and spending power; cheap finance is available to firms and this boosts supply across the whole economy.

Soon after the Big Bang, the Conservatives cut the top rate of income tax from 60% to 40%. Above the top earnings threshold, therefore, workers were taxed by only 40p in each £1 instead of 60p. This boosted aggregate demand significantly (and helped fuel unsustainable increases in shares and house prices) but the key benefit has been the increase in incentives such a cut in taxes brings. The higher the marginal rate of income tax, the less incentive a worker has to find and keep a job. Economists disagree on the relative benefits of low taxes (which boost incentives) versus high taxes (which can be used to redistribute income and reduce inequality) but no government since the reduction in 1987 has chosen to increase the top rate of tax, although it could be argued that the present government has, until recently, increased the threshold by less than inflation each year – sucking more workers into the top rate of income tax in the process.

Income tax rates affect the incentives of workers, and corporation taxes (taxes on business profits) affect the incentives of entrepreneurs. If entrepreneurs are allowed to keep a higher proportion of their profits (through lower corporation tax rates) it is argued that they will seek to expand their businesses (increasing employment in the process) and, again, the supply-side of the economy expands.

Gordon Brown, in his last Budget as Chancellor in 2007, reduced UK corporation tax from 30% to 28%. In an increasingly global world economy, such a move aims to attract international business as well as to increase incentives to existing domestic suppliers.

Governments sometimes appear to pursue contradictory policies, for example setting a target of 50% of school-leavers into higher education (particularly aiming to increase the proportion of students from lower income backgrounds), but also introducing tuition fees, which could act as a disincentive to potential students (particularly those from lower income backgrounds!)

Note that there can be an overlap between fiscal policy and supply-side policy. Fiscal policy is usually used to describe short-run attempts to control the economy through aggregate demand, and supply-side policy the long-run impacts on the PPF and LRAS.

Problems with supply-side policy

The main limitation of supply-side policy is the long *time lags* involved. Cuts in tax rates can change behaviour, but it may take time for this to feed into higher growth and job creation. Education policy (e.g. attempting to improve primary school literacy) should boost the future skills of the workforce, but it may be years or even decades before those children become productive members of the workforce.

Another problem is that supply-side policy may simply not work and higher spending may not increase output. This could be because, say, educational reform does not improve standards, or because the government cannot give the same incentives to entrepreneurs as the profit motive. In addition, the theory of crowding-out (see Chapter 8, Fiscal Policy) suggests that higher government spending and intervention in the economy may simply reduce private sector investment. Thus, as AD = C + I + G + (X-M), the increase in government spending (G) is balanced out by lower investment (I).

Public Choice Theory dismisses as unrealistic the idea that public officials will always seek to maximise social welfare. The theory argues that governments aim to maximise votes to gain re-election, and will thus choose popular rather than painful policies, even when this has serious implications for long-run economic growth. The persistent underfunding of the transport infrastructure is a typical example.

Summary questions

1. Distinguish between supply-side growth and supply-side policy.

2. Why is productivity an important measure of economic performance?

3. Using a diagram, show how supply-side growth can limit inflationary pressure during a boom.

4. Using examples, explain how the government can boost the supply-side performance of the macroeconomy?

5. Why are successful supply-side policies difficult to implement?

Extension questions

A. How do higher participation rates affect the UK labour market and the UK economy?

B. 'The long-run impact of low taxes is more important than the short-run impact on aggregate demand.' To what extent do you agree with this statement?

C. Evaluate the success of supply-side policy in the UK since 1997.

Chapter 10

The UK Economy: an overview

Growth, jobs and prices: the big three

The UK economy enjoyed strong and stable growth between recovering from recession in the early 1990s and the credit and economic problems arising since August 2007. Some – if not all – of this growth has been attributed to successful macroeconomic management of both the demand- and supply-side of the economy. Economic growth created jobs and UK unemployment fell and, until recently, remained low. Even successful economies in the 21st Century will experience job destruction as well as job creation – a strong economy therefore balances the loss of employment (due to changes in industrial structure, world demand, and shifts in patterns of world production) with new opportunities for labour in growing industries. Providing job creation does not fall below job destruction there should be no major increase in unemployment.

The NICE decade

The period of low-inflationary growth from the mid-1990s to 2007 has come to be known as the NICE decade: an acronym for Non-Inflationary Constant Expansion. Of particular interest to economists is the phenomenon of low-inflationary growth. Despite strong growth in GDP, price inflation remained under control, suggesting that there was sufficient supply-side growth to balance strong demand.

The key factors keeping inflation low during the NICE decade were:

1. *Policy independence for the Bank of England:* the specific targeting of inflation by interest rates has helped to reduce inflationary pressures when necessary, and lowered inflationary expectations in general.

2. *Labour immigration:* migrant workers may be willing to work for lower wages than incumbents in the UK labour market, and their presence also keeps wage demands low in industries where domestic workers feel they could be replaced easily by foreign workers.

3. *Supply-side growth:* increased participation rates by some groups of workers (e.g. working mothers and students) and lower trade union power since the reforms of the 1980s. Successive governments have attempted to provide businesses with a dynamic and competitive environment.

4. *Cheap imported goods:* particularly from newly industrialising economies such as China as they opened up to more trade with the world economy. In addition to lowering the price of some goods, this increased competition has also forced Western businesses to find ways of cutting costs (e.g. outsourcing some or all of production to less developed countries) and passing on these savings to consumers in the form of lower prices. Strong sterling for much of the NICE decade was also a factor in keeping the price of imports low.

5. *Cheap and easy credit:* one feature of the growth of emerging economies has been the current account surpluses run by countries such as China. Saving ratios are far higher in these economies than in, for example, the UK and USA, and thus the movement of currency from low saving to high saving countries has increased the global supply of money. This was an important factor in providing cheap and easy lending during the NICE decade.

Twin deficits: the other two macroeconomic objectives

The experience of the USA and UK were similar during the NICE years with both economies enjoying stable growth alongside low unemployment and low inflation. In the USA, and the UK to a lesser extent, this was achieved alongside deteriorating positions on both the current account and the budget. Growth can be achieved through both demand- and supply-side means, but where demand is allowed to grow at unsustainable levels this tends to increase imports above exports: put simply, the economy is spending too much and producing too little. This causes the current account deficit to grow and both the UK and USA have seen large deficits emerge. The risks associated with this phenomenon are controversial and were touched on in Chapter 5.

Figure 10.1: US and UK current account, % of GDP

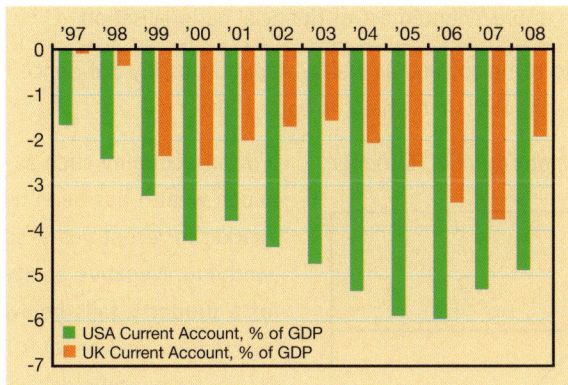

Source: ONS & BEA

Where the problem can deepen is if the growth has been created, in part, through a budget deficit: usually a combination of lower taxation and higher spending which has boosted aggregate demand. The UK tried to avoid this problem through Gordon Brown's Code for Fiscal Stability ('fiscal rules') which aimed to limit both current expenditure (through the golden rule) and capital expenditure (through the sustainable investment rule). Gordon Brown's interpretation of an economic cycle – when it begins and ends – was criticised by some as a way of fudging a failure to meet his own golden rule, and the credit crisis of 2008 put both rules under great pressure.

In addition to problems with deficits, inflationary pressures in the UK have grown as CPI inflation moved above the top boundary of 3% in April 2008 and, since September 2008, has actually been higher than the RPI measure. Some economists have argued that the long period of low interest rates and easy credit availability from the mid-1990s onwards stoked housing market inflation and allowed household debt to rise to dangerous levels. The housing market boom of the 1990s saw higher house prices increase the wealth of home-owning households, pushing consumption upwards and fuelling demand in the economy. However, a warning sign was present in the form of the saving ratio (see Figure 10.2).

Figure 10.2: UK saving ratio (% of disposable income saved)

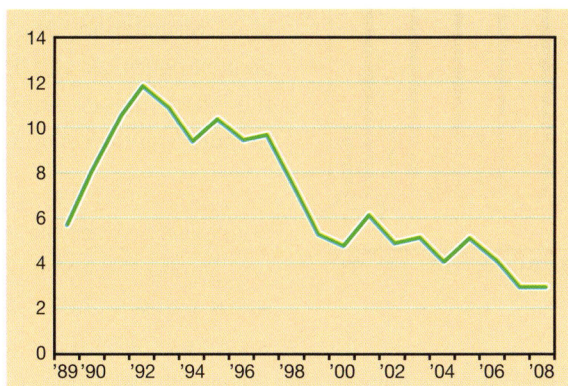

Source: ONS

The absence of traditional saving during the NICE decade is of particular concern. In 1991 and 1992, when the UK last experienced recession, the saving ratio was rising as households presumably prepared for a difficult period of slowing growth. As incomes rise, it is usual for households to increase both saving and consumption, but it appears that households are less well-prepared for recession this time; with sharp falls in house prices and stock markets, household wealth has fallen dramatically and, as unemployment rises, the housing market could see further falls as homeowners are unable to meet mortgage payments and banks repossess their property. Without sufficient savings to cope with unemployment or falls in real income due to inflation, many households could face the prospect of genuine poverty and hardship.

The Credit Crunch

The Credit Crunch began in earnest, arguably, on August 9th 2008 when concerns regarding the exposure of some banks to bad debt began to dramatically increase the global cost of credit. A slowdown in the US housing market exposed lenders to the possibility of serious losses, compounded by previous lending to households with significant risk of default ('subprime' borrowers) and the repackaging of this high risk debt as low risk securities which had been extensively traded throughout the world financial system.

The prospect of serious losses forced banks to dramatically increase the interest rates they charged when lending to each other (the LIBOR rate), and consequently to businesses and households. This exposed those banks which were heavily dependent on funds from credit markets, and high profile cases such as Northern Rock and Bradford and Bingley in the UK saw the government step in to take control and guarantee savers' deposits in an unprecedented act of financial nationalisation.

The shortage of funds available to borrowers, as well as rapid drops in confidence in the UK housing market, saw house prices fall for the first time since the early 1990s..

Figure 10.3: Halifax house price index (annual % change)

Source: Lloyds Banking Group

For an economy such as the UK, where so much wealth has been held in the housing market in recent years, such a trend is very worrying. Negative equity (where the value of a property falls below the outstanding mortgage owed on it) is likely to become a reality for households and a negative wealth effect is likely to reduce spending further – probably creating a downward spiral in the market. In addition, significant losses on stock exchanges around the world have reduced the wealth of savers holding shares.

With the benefit of hindsight... 2009 and beyond

Figure 10.4: UK aggregate demand, 1998-2008, £bn

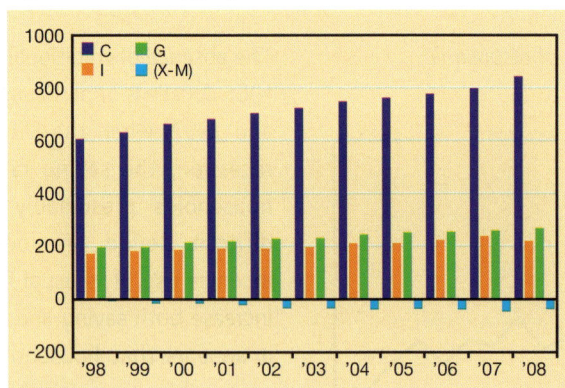

Source: ONS

Figure 10.4 clearly illustrates the consumer-led boom of the NICE decade: investment and government spending grew slightly over this period, but the main source of rising GDP was consumption. The growing current account deficit can also be seen as (X-M) on the chart moves further into negative territory over the period shown.

A common problem in macroeconomics is to distinguish between the short-run and long-run. During the boom periods of the late 1990s and early 2000s there was a genuine, widespread belief that countries such as the UK and USA could create highly successful economies using the opportunities created by globalisation in the manufacturing, transport and financial sectors to produce consistently high economic growth without the previous problems of the 'boom-and-bust' economic cycle. Costs were falling: in credit markets, goods markets and commodity markets, and supply-side expansion allowed non-inflationary growth.

As the world economy adapts to the Credit Crunch and the possibility of slowdowns in emerging economies and threat of greater protectionism, another chapter of the story of the world economy will be written. It seems clear, already, that deflationary pressures and higher costs of credit have taken their toll on economic agents from the individual household and firm to the governments of most world powers.

Reasons to be cheerful?

Figure 10.5: Sterling exchange rate, versus US Dollar and Euro

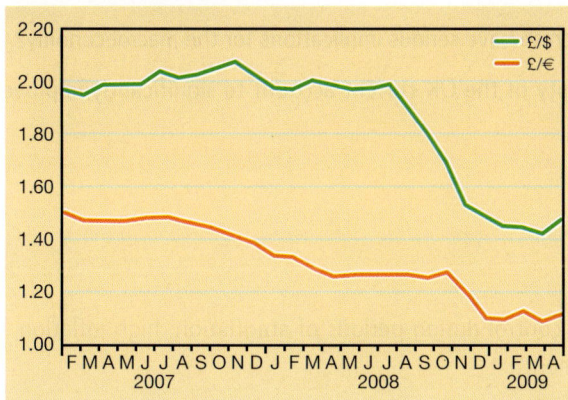

Source: HM Treasury

The value of sterling in foreign exchange markets has fallen as the UK economy has entered recession and the UK financial sector has experienced severe problems as a result of the Credit Crunch. This may help the UK economy in the medium- to long-term as weaker sterling benefits exporters and limits demand for imports when domestic substitutes are available. This raises key questions for the UK economy in 2009 and beyond: to what extent can a decline in consumer spending be offset by other domestic components of aggregate demand (increased investment seems unlikely in a difficult business environment, but the use of Keynesian-style deficit spending has been used by the UK government); and, will a weaker currency boost aggregate demand through redressing recent imbalances in the value of exports versus the value of imports?

Hope may be offered using historic data for the UK from before the NICE decade: between 1993 and 1997 the UK enjoyed positive real growth alongside falling inflation and an improvement in the current account. This was caused by the depreciation of sterling when the UK left the Exchange Rate Mechanism (ERM) in September 1992 which was initially regarded as an economic disaster, but which proved beneficial as the UK experienced export-led growth with consumption and investment driven, in part, by the stimulus of an improving current account position.

Figure 10.6: Pre-NICE – UK real growth, inflation and current account, 1991-1997

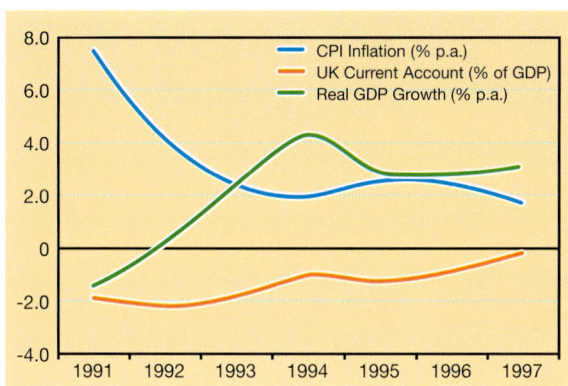

Source: ONS

Of course, the UK and world economy are facing different issues as the 21st century approaches its second decade. For students of macroeconomics, the subject is as exciting and important as ever. To echo an ancient Chinese curse: 'May you live in interesting times.'

Summary questions

1. To what extent does recent UK economic experience support the traditional link between growth, inflation and unemployment?

2. How would you expect the cost-push and demand-pull pressures on UK inflation to change in the next 18 months?

3. 'Depreciation of sterling and the US dollar is inevitable in the light of recent events.' To what extent do you agree with this statement?

4. Why does a housing market crash have serious implications for the macroeconomy?

5. What could limit the possibility of the UK current account to significantly improve if sterling weakens?

Extension questions

A. Which is more important to control during periods of stagflation: high inflation, or slowing growth and rising unemployment?

B. In light of your answer to A, what policy(s) would you propose?

C. Keynes referred to 'animal spirits' to help explain the tendency for economies to experience booms followed by recessions. How helpful is this term in explaining recent events in the world economy?